Title: Money Is Freedom.
Author: Gert J.R. van Niekerk

ISBN: 9798201206215

This is not a "How to get Rich Book" there are enough of them-this book is about Financial Survival and Monetary Peace of Mind

Shortage of Money

And

Retirement Comes In A Wink!!!

So, Start To

Plan and Budget Immediately!!!

To be able to

Survive

Foreword
Written By
Gert van Niekerk

It is a given that in more and more countries the state pensions that are paid out to individuals isn't adequate for its pensioners to survive on, let alone live the retirement life that they, the pensioners, have waited for their whole working life.

It is a given that, because on average people live longer and the skilled population stays stable or have a negative growth, more and more countries will allow the working population to work longer before state retirement pensions are being paid out as to offset the increase in state spending on more and more pensioners.

The cost of living all over the world is spiralling upward at such a rate that only those who study the value of money and methods of creating proper retirement provision will be able to have a comfortable or at least survivable life and retirement!

Only people who set definite Monetary Targets, Plan and Budget to reach those targets will be able to retire!

To retire comfortably you should have, at least, saved twelve (12) times your last year's or annual salary or lifestyle income.

I wrote this book for the younger generation and the majority of working people on earth knowing nothing or little, or are ignorant about the financial world around them.

I studied first year Economics, Commercial Law, Industrial Economics, Statistics and Accountancy at university but I cannot say that I am highly educated in financials or economics nor did I do in-depth studies of these subjects as I wanted to write this book out of a general working person's perspective and practical Life Experience.

This book is not "How to Get Rich" but rather "How to Survive" and then maybe have a basis to someday get rich. The military forces teach their personnel survival skills because they realise that to go into high risk defensive or offensive operational mode successfully, you must be able to survive-as a priority.

But how can money give one "Freedom"?

Read the book and take special note of the final chapter named "Closing".

Acknowledgements.

A great thank you to my dear farther and mother (Gert and Katrina), not with us anymore, who taught me good manners, discipline, compassion and tried hard to instil neatness in my daily life-although not fully successful with the neatness.

Through example they laid the foundation of realising the value of money.

As our family was working class and my parents could very seldom afford expensive toys and gifts at various occasions, they never realised the impact of the Meccano set, oil paint set, chemical set and the books they gave me had and have on my life.

A great thank you to my dear sister, who was a successful retired school teacher and active at the age of seventy three adjudicating drama competitions, Dina, who knowingly or unknowingly taught me diligence in studying, good administration and the general approach to schooling. I must humbly admit that, due to my farther working long hours and my mother just being to gentle and a softy, my sister was solely responsible for getting me through primary school-sometimes at the wooden end of a feather duster.

I shall never forget the love me and my late wife René, a very dedicated school teacher by profession, shared for the various art forms and always being inspirational to each other.

Above all I must have a special acknowledgement for my two children **Adelé** and Rudolph who through very trying times stood by me and with gentleness; diligence and shear persistence successfully completed their schooling and obtained their degrees and diplomas at university.

In my life I had many role models such as family, teachers, friends, national and international leaders, working colleagues and seniors who were worthy of observance for leadership and learning from.

I do not want to make any exceptions but if it comes to languages and for an inspiration for writing, I must make an exception for two of my teachers at the Technical College Langlaagte in Johannesburg namely Dr. Rautenbagh (Afrikaans) and Mister J.Loots (English). These two teachers, who weren't always impressed with my ability and use of general grammar, always complemented me on my poetry, comprehension and composition work.

I always got in the higher 90%s for my compositions which was mostly due to their inspiration, assistance and freedom they allowed me to express myself.

Introduction

I, like millions of people on this earth is reaching my late fifties and realize, although I made provision for my retirement, that I have to make very accurate calculations and decisions as to be in a much better financial position when I reach the magic retirement age of sixty five.

It is well known that the average lifespan of us human beings have risen to almost seventy five years in the western world. This was brought about by dramatic advancement and the improvement of the medical, food, transport, employment, housing and a multitude of other technologies and sciences.

<u>A major factor which is generally not recognised is that on average woman live longer than men, therefore all women must be more conscious of their money matters and retirement planning than ever before!</u>

Very quickly various people would say "why worry about it, be happy that there is a chance that everybody is going to live longer and why be so silly as to want to write a book about it!"

The reality of today is and it will be increasingly so in the future, that more people are going to need more money for **much longer** and that it is going to require much more energy, planning, monetary discipline, focusing on personal financial planning and money awareness!

Why????

It is well known that the majority of people are employed by a corporate or business and the self employed peoples make out a small percentage of the work force, thus most of us and our futures whether skilled or unskilled, educated or uneducated are literary in the hands of these corporates!

Over the world the corporate/ business, employment strategies and methodologies have changed dramatically!

Due to various factors, like maximum company profits, the stringency of cost control, shareholders pressure on companies for higher returns on investment, government policy changes, competition in the employment market and a host of other influences have had a major impact on the way of how individuals structure their financial lives as to financially survive and to prepare for their retirement.

Gone are the days when most people start employment at a certain company and retire

within this company on a pension fund that pays out a liveable lump sum and monthly pension which will last for the rest of your life.

As earlier mentioned the maximum profit' motive have become so intense that buzz words like corporate restructuring, contract employment, company mergers, company takeovers, company liquidations, company competition, fraud, shareholders expectation on investment return and bad business management in companies have the direct effect of

retrenchments and layoffs of employees without proper time and money considerations to the employees by most companies.

It is a fact that ninety percent of all employees in the capitalist or western world will

be retrenched, fired or simply shut out from employment two or three times during their working lives with highly detrimental financial loss and with detrimental impact on their retirement planning.

So what is the purpose of this book and what qualifies the author to write it?

The main purpose of this book is to sensitise the readers of the fact that retirement will be upon you much faster than you can imagine, all prices of all life essentials are continuously rising and that **financial budgeting** for the inevitable event will have to be a **major part** of your planning and everybody on earth wanting even just financially survive will have to master the art of financial planning.

Most people my age, **I am Sixty Six**, have experienced and learned many facets of life of which the financial aspects are very relevant. We have made many financial mistakes of our own doing and those which have been thrust or forced upon us without expecting or anticipating it. There are also many financial principals and decisions which was followed and made correctly.

Due to growing up in a home with parents who weren't rich but very hardworking and loving I had to leave school without completing the last school year. Through perseverance and night school I completed my high school, completed a trade apprenticeship, obtained college and university diplomas and have a moderate but good education.

I wrote this book mainly to advise as many a person to do their utmost to plan, budget, organize, calculate and be in deep thought about retirement and financial security on a day to day basis and as soon in your lives as possible <u>which means start now! You must have enough money to survive in Normal circumstances, for the Unforeseen which will cross your life's path and to enjoy the fruits of your hard labour!</u>

I have written the book mainly out of a South African perspective but the principals stay the same all over the world.

The money unit used is South African Rand but these can be changed with US Dollar, Pounds, and Euros, Yen or any other currency which is in use with the reader.

The older persons in our families use to say "turn a penny/cent twice before you spend it."

I say "turn a penny Five Times, think while you are turning it and then you will know how to spend it wisely and most probably with a profit."

Gert van Niekerk

Contents

Chapter 1

<u>What is Personal Financial Planning?</u>

Because I am not an economist or a high profile financial advisor I write in layman terms. Spending my entire life in engineering and project management I have the advantage off being able to convert the theoretical into the practical world.

Generally most people do know what planning is and practices it every day but refuse to utilize this instrument when it comes to the more serious matters such as financial planning, health planning, house buying, buying an automobile, education planning e.t.c., all of which is part of your Personal Financial Planning.

<u>Planning is simply taking every aspect of all actions into organised consideration to ensure reaching a set goal with a satisfying result</u>. (There are millions of definitions for planning but I try to keep it practical)

Example: If you go on a holiday you do not jump in your car, onto a bus, aircraft or any form of transport, head into any direction with the hope of finding accommodation and then expect you and your family to have an enjoyable holiday!!

No, you always meticulously plan every aspect of the holiday.

Advanced leave provisions from work or profession, advanced booking of accommodation, booking transport, servicing the car, getting roadmaps, deciding on clothing, making money provisions are but a few of the aspects which are planned for the holiday.

We also plan for all short term activities like buying groceries, entertainment, getting to work, dropping the children at school painting the house and so forth.

But do we budget all of the above to know what the monetary effect will be?

Do we have a proper budget to see if we can afford it **Without** going into **Credit** and what the long term personal **Money** effect will be?

Fail to Plan and YOU Plan to Fail.

Personal financial planning is no different from corporate financial planning in that the company must be solvent e.g. be able to do business, survive in the corporate world, fulfil its obligations of paying its employees and creditors, expanding and above all to reach the company's set <u>goals.</u>

Why are there so many successful businesses and certain individuals in the world and yet there are hundreds of millions of poor people who live in absolute misery?

It is very simple – all businesses big or small **<u>and individuals</u>** must plan. Those who plan correctly survive and grow to be more successful, those who plan incorrectly barely survive or disappear, those who do not plan, hardly come of the ground and do not survive.

<u>**The same principals apply to All Individuals!**</u>

But, everybody everywhere will say, availability of usable money is the key for success and few realize that money is one of the most important factors in our lives from the day we are born to the day that we die **<u>and even after our deaths!!</u>**

So it is of the utmost importance that we manage our money in a disciplined, focused and responsible way and planning is a key element in your management system.

The rules for personal finance are the same as for business finance namely to first survive and grow and then to be prosperous or happy, content, secure, rich or whatever your aim, goal or ambition.

Why am I rambling about every thing if the purpose of this book is to "Plan For Retirement Now! "

Simple:

- All of us are going to grow up and leave school.

- Ninety nine percent of us are going to make

Money somehow, to survive and or prosper.

- Most of us are going to pay Income tax.
- All of us must eat and have to feed our families.
- All of us must have clothes.
- All of us must have a place to live.
- (with everything that we must have for living)
- Most of us marry and have children.
- **<u>All of us must grow old and retire from direct money making activities.</u>**
- All of us are going to get medical treatment throughout our lives and more so the older we get.
- **<u>All of us are going to die.</u>**
- All of us are going to leave a family behind when we died.

<u>**Financial Planning.**</u>

<u>Financial Planning is simply taking every monetary/ Money aspect of all income (Plus Money) and expenditure(Minus Money) actions into thorough and organised consideration to ensure reaching the goal of financial independence and money freedom, especially in view of your retirement one day</u>.(There are millions of definitions for financial planning but I am trying to keep it practical)

A few pointers

This book is not for the already rich because they have planned and budgeted and is, busy planning and budgeting to get even richer!!

This book is not for the how to get rich either.

This book is about first surviving then be financially secure then being financially independent and then have money freedom during your life and retirement and maybe getting rich in the process.

We are continuously bombarded by the advertising media, banks, insurance companies, financial advisors, investment companies, stock exchange agents, property agents, medical schemes on how, where and when to invest and save but no one or no company or bank will tell you to make sure that you must have the **Money for all these fabulous investments.**

At one stage I found that I have virtually invested myself into bankruptcy!

Why, because I did not make sure that I had enough **Money** for all these investments, I did not make sure that the investments were affordable, or that some of these investments e.g. my retirement annuities did not pay out as much as the projections that the life policy company projected of what it will pay out.

I know that the readers, at this stage will tell me "please Gert van Niekerk tell us what is personal financial planning!"

Again, although for me in hindsight, it is simply thinking of how you have used, is using and are going to use your money to your best interest and for your best future.

With other words plan your financial matters as if you are planning a well organized holiday with special emphasis on a good road map which you made sure you understand.

Make sure that you know how much money you have and what your capabilities /power/controls are with that money.

Make sure that you make provision for you life's journey and also for the successful stay at your retirement.

But how do we know how to plan and anticipate so far ahead and what tools do we use to accomplish our goals?

The most power full tool to accomplish money matters and control it, lies in the art of managing a **budget** and that **is the primary target of this book and what this book is about.**

The secondary target is to give a step by step, chapter by chapter layout and advice of the minimum detail which must be in your budget.

Chapter 2
What Is A Budget

2.1 <u>Meaning of the Word "Budget."</u>

There are various meanings, layouts and definitions for a budget, but lets first of all look what the dictionaries say and in particular "The Concise Oxford Dictionary".

Budget:

- **Annual estimate of revenue and expenditure of a country or organization.**
- **Private person's or family's similar estimate of an amount of money needed or available.**
- **Inexpensive.**
- **Avoiding undue expense.**
- **Account plan(with revolving credit and regular payments)**

See how clearly the explanations summarise into **"Plan <u>Income</u> and <u>Expenditure</u>"**

It almost correlates with the laws of Physics, Common Law and so forth, e.g.

Physics- For every Action there will be a direct and opposite Reaction.

Common Law- Every human have Rights but every right also have Obligations within those rights.

Summary.

A Budget Teach and Help you to:

- **Have control over your money;**
- **To constantly see what your money status/position is;**
- **Make you see what the possibilities for the future is;**

- **A budget teaches you to <u>Save</u> ; and above all**
- **Not to <u>Waste</u>.**

2.2 <u>Physical Budget.</u>

Figure 1 is just a very basic example of what your budget will evolve from.

Your budget must be on a recoverable document or computer file, do not scribble it on pieces of paper or unsaved files as it must be a daily working document such as those controlled by the company charted accountant or the military general!

The best way to draw up a Budget Matrix is on your lap top or desk computer- Microsoft Excel is a perfect program to construct you budget as you can enter the necessary formulas to do the calculations for you.

<u>Remember that the purpose of your budget is to:</u>

- Set yourself a realistic and reachable target e.g. "I must draw up a plan to help me accumulate$/ R 200,000-00 in my savings account so as to give me enough credibility at my bank for a home loan/bond and a buffer for the unexpected"

- Plan your financial status (your money value) for specific use over a certain period.(Draft plan)
- This plan will show you whether you have the money to execute or afford the plan.(Investigate and Feasibility)
- You will immediately see how and where the plan must be changed and adjusted as to be <u>affordable.(Final plan from which you must not allow yourself to deviate)</u>
- **A budget plan forces you to tell the <u>truth</u> to yourself and your family about the state of your finances.**

<u>Draft Budget for Sue and Joe Watson. Budget Year 1</u>

Item Description	Jan 14	Feb 14	March 14	April 14	May 14	June 14	
Income (Plus Money)							
1. Salary Joe	5000	5000	5000	5000	5000	5000	
1. Salary Sue	3500	3500	3500	3500	3500	3500	
1. Profit, Joe's Small Computer Business	1500	1500	1500	1500	1500	1500	
1. Profit, Sue's Small Garment Business	1200	1200	1200	1200	1200	1200	
5. Interest From Savings Account	650	650	650	650	650	650	
Month Total Income	11850	11850	11850	11850	11850	1185	
B)							
Expenditure (MinusMoney)							
1) Food & Groceries	1100	1100	1100	1100	1100	1100	11
2) Home Rental	2250	2250	2250	2250	2250	2250	22
3) Telephone Bill	300	300	300	300	300	300	30
4) Water, Electricity	1100	1100	1100	1100	1100	1100	11
5) Rates & Taxes	380	380	380	380	380	380	38
6) Provision Clothes	250	250	250	250	250	250	25
7) Joe's Car Instalment	1500	1500	1500	1500	2200	2200	22
8) Sue's Car Instalment	850	850	850	850	850	850	85
9) Savings Account	1500	1500	1500	1500	1500	1500	15

Month Total Expend.	9280	9980	9280	9280	9980	9980	9980
Income Minus Expenditure.	2570	2570	2570	2570	1870	1870	1870

Note: the negative (Minus or -) figures in your budget indicates that you are going into a situation where you do not or will not have money to pay for the items in your budget. So you must urgently make plans to reduce spending to go into a positive (Plus or +) situation.

Joe and Sue have drawn up a **Draft budget plan** for one (1) year to see if the new home/apartment and two automobiles they plan to buy will fit into their Budget.(to see if they will have the **money to do what they want to do.**)

From the Draft budget Joe and Sue can clearly see:

- **Expenditure exceeds their income by 270 Rands, US Dollars, Euro or whatever from September. With other words they can not afford the two new automobiles and new home.**
- **Their monthly Income minus Expenditure e.g. their monthly profit is turned into a loss-but where did the money go to?**
- **Between them they have R130, 000-00 in their Special savings accounts!**

What are they to do about it? Here are a few golden rules!

- Do not try to compete with the "Joneses" next door, friends or your family, they are either rich, most probably live the luxury life with high risk credit or financially planned correctly and not they the banks or anybody will help you if in serious financial trouble!
- Be **truthful** to yourself and your family and realize that you **cannot afford** that expensive house/apartment and two expensive automobiles.
- Go into a credit situation for only your own home and automobile and get out of it as soon as possible!

Joe and Sue also realized the following while drawing up the Draft Budget:

Income (Plus Money)

Salary Joe.

A salary increase of minimum R500-00p.m. is due in December 2006.

A yearly bonus is of R5000-00 is due in December 2006.

Salary Sue.

A salary increase of minimum R350-00p.m. is due in December 2006.

A yearly bonus is of R3500-00 is due in December 2006.

Expenditure (Minus Money)

Food & Groceries

They forgot to budget for the baby which is on its way! The food and grocery bill will increase by at least R500-00 p.m.

Home Rental

The home rental will increase by 10% representing an additional expenditure of R250-00p.m.

Telephone Bill

By using the telephone more during call more/ low cost periods of the day and not as frequent and unnecessary long periods.

Cell phones or mobile phones, as the Americans call it, are the most convenient and usable instruments of our century but do not let it become an absolute financial burden.

With Blackberries, Tablets, Smart Phones and a host of other phone instruments manufacturers, distributers and retailers make billions upon bullions out of millions and millions of people and there families!

Remember that if you just have an ordinary low cost cell/mobile phone for basic use you can get all the information or data you need from your television, radio stations, internet, news papers, magazines and libraries.

Why pay over and over for the same thing!!!!

The manufacturers, distributers and retailers make billions upon bullions out of millions and millions of people and there families- and they just love it making us pay over and over for the same things!

<u>Water, Electricity Bill</u>

By utilizing the electricity tips which nowadays are so continuously and widely published by the media and discussed by engineers and scientists a fair share of your water and electricity bills can be saved.

<u>Joe's Car Instalment</u>

They realized that his car is still in a good condition very comfortable, will be paid of by November 2006 and with the proper maintenance will easily last another two years , will still have a reasonable resale value and will bring in a saving of R1500-00p.m.

<u>Sue's Car Instalment</u>

They realized that her car is still in a good condition very and comfortable, will be paid of by November 2013 and with the proper maintenance will easily last another two years, will still have a reasonable resale value and will bring in a saving of R850-00p.m.

<u>Savings Account</u>

Remember that money paid into a savings account is not an expenditure or liability but an asset (Plus Money), but keep it there as to force yourself to save diligently.

<u>Income Minus Expenditure (Profit/Loss)</u>

Joe and Sue, at first, could not believe that they have R2600-00 left at the end of each month and analysed it.

They found the following:

- Takeaway food twice a week = at least R800-00p.m.
- Eating at the restaurant once a week = at least R800-00p.m.
- One getaway holiday weekend every three months = R900-00p.m.
- **By cutting down considerably on, but not going without it**

at least R1500-00 will be saved!

For the purpose of this book I shall not go into the difficult calculations of Mark up, Gross profit, Nett profit, profit percentages, cash flow, input and output percentages and so forth.

I shall use profit simply in the context of money which we have extra and can be saved or be used other than paying for some forced expenditure.

<u>On the findings from their Draft Budget Joe and Sue decided the following:</u>

- They will drive their present cars for another two years.
- Only buy a house in January 2016.
- Drastically cut down on takeaways and restaurant lunches.
- Cut down on holiday weekends.
- Put the savings from these actions into their special savings account.
- Draw up final budgets for 2015.

Here are their new and final budget for 2015.

<u>Budget Year 2.</u>

Item Description	Jan 15	Feb 15	March 15	April 15	May 15	June 15	July 15	Aug 15
Income (Plus Money)								
Salary Joe	5000	5000	5000	5000	5000	5000	5000	500
Salary Sue	3500	3500	3500	3500	3500	3500	3500	350
Income, Joe's Small	1500	1500	1500	1500	1500	1500	1500	150
Computer Business								
Income, Sue's Small	1200	1200	1200	1200	1200	1200	1200	120
Garment Business								
Interest From Savings Account	50	50	50	50	50	50	50	50
Month Total Income	11850	11850	11850	11850	11850	11850	11850	118
B)								
Expenditure(Minus Money)								
Food & Groceries	1600	1600	1600	1600	1600	1600	1600	1600

Home Rental	2250	2250	2250	2250	2250	2250	2250	22
Telephone Bill	275	275	275	275	275	275	275	27
Water, Electricity	1100	1100	1100	1100	1100	1100	1100	11
Rates & Taxes	380	380	380	380	380	380	380	38
Provision Clothes	250	250	250	250	250	250	250	25
Joe's Car Instalment	1500	1500	1500	1500	1500	1500	1500	15
Sue's Car Instalment	850	850	850	850	850	850	850	85
Savings Account	500	500	500	500	500	500	500	50
Month Total Expend.	11705	11705	11705	11705	11705	11705	11705	11
Income Minus Expenditure.	1145	1145	1145	1145	1145	1145	1145	11

Note: the negative (Minus or -) figures in your budget indicates that you are going into a situation where you do not or will not have money to pay for the items in your budget. So you must urgently make plans to reduce spending to go into a positive (Plus or +) situation.

It can clearly be seen that by making a few minor adjustments to their life styles and not withstanding the normal increases in food, home rental and other expenses Joe and Sue can in 2015:

- **Save an extra R1145-00 p.m.;**
- **Still enjoy the regular takeaway food, some entertainment, restaurant lunch; and**
- **The greatest aspect of this budget is that the special savings account will grow from R130, 000-00 in 2014 to approximately R145, 000-00 by the end of 2015 with bank interest.**

The money in the special savings account will:

- **Give them easier access to a home loan;**
- **It can be given as an deposit on the new home thus reducing the bond repayments; or**
- **Use the interest from the special savings account to increase the bond repayments which will have the effect of earning more than double the interest on these savings over the medium to long term and shortening the bond repayment period substantially.(Not a great step but a huge leap toward Money freedom and Sleeping without money worries!)**
- **Remember that buying your own home is in itself an asset and a savings vehicle!**

Let us have a look at how their budget will look for 2007(Figure 3)

2015. Final Budget. Figure 3 Note: I included a salary increase only for example purposes refer salary chapter 3.

Item Description	Jan 15	Feb 15	March 15	April 15	May 15	June 15	July 15
Income (Plus Money)							
Salary Joe	5500	5500	5500	5500	5500	5500	550(
Salary Sue	3850	3850	3850	3850	3850	3850	385(
Income, Joe's Small Computer Business	1500	1500	1500	1500	1500	1500	150(
Income, Sue's Small Garment Business	1200	1200	1200	1200	1200	1200	120(
Interest From Savings Account.	950	950	950	950	950	950	100(
Month Total Income	13000	13000	13000	13000	13000	13000	130(
B) Expenditure(Minus Money)							
Food & Groceries	1750	1750	1750	1750	1750	1750	1750	1
Home Bond Payment	4000	4000	4000	4000	4000	4000	4000	4
Telephone Bill	303	303	303	303	303	303	303	3
Water, Electricity	1210	1210	1210	1210	1210	1210	1210	1
Rates & Taxes	380	380	380	380	380	380	380	3
Provision Clothes	250	250	250	250	250	250	250	2
Joe's Car Instalment	0	0	0	0	0	0	0	0
Sue's Car Instalment	0	0	0	0	0	0	0	0
Savings Account	3500	3500	3500	3500	3500	3500	3500	3
Month Total Expend.	11393	11393	11393	11393	11393	11393	11393	1
Income Minus	1607	1607	1607	1607	1607	1607	1607	1

Expenditure(Profit/Loss)

The positives can be seen clearly, now the acid test will be to execute and live in accordance with the **<u>Budget!!!!!</u>**

Chapter 3
Essentials in Financial Life.

3.1 Income. (Inflow of Plus Money)

Introduction.

3.1.1 Your Salary or Enumeration

3.1.2 Income from Small Business

3.1.3 Income from Savings

3.1.4 Income from Pension Fund

3.1.5 Inheritances

3.1.6 Income from Additional Property

3.1.7 Income From Shares (Stock Market)

3.1.8 Valuables

3.1.9 Income Tax

3.1.10 Profit

3.1 Income. (Inflow of Plus Money)

Everybody Today, Must Have Sufficient Money Income As to Pay and Save For The Needs Of Today and Of Tomorrow!!!!

Please note that income, for the purposes of this book, describes any money which is coming to you from any and all sources as to allow you to pay for food, housing clothing any debt, credit, outstanding amounts **and most of all yourself.**

Interest from savings will be seen as an income whatever your intentions are with the money.

Weekly or monthly savings placed in to any savings vehicle whether an savings account, retirement annuity, pension fund, bond savings account, shareholdings or what ever will be seen as an expenditure because you must see yourself as one of your most important creditors-you must simply make provision to pay yourself!

If you do not have a Money Income you will not have the means to have food, clothing, home, an automobile or any of the necessities of life!

Banks, building societies or any of the financial institutions will NOT lend you any money for Anything if you cannot give them proof of a stable Income!

All these institutions want you to prove that you are able to pay them back and with interest! They want to minimize their risk or do not want any risk at all.

Remember that all the financial institutions want and must make money and interest and profits from that money!

So you must have an Income whether it is from:

- **Your Salary or Enumeration;**
- **Income from Small Business/Business;**
- **Income from Savings;**

- **Income from Pension Fund;**
- **Inheritances;**
- **Income from Additional Property;**
- **Income from Taxation; or**
- **Any other legal means!**

The basic message is that the more Savings you have, in what ever form, and the more stable Income you have the more you will be able to reach the higher use of financial institutions money to your own advantage until you do not have to use them anymore and

reach higher and higher levels of:

These paragraphs is very important for you and your family's future.

3.1.1 Enumeration or Salary.

Most people when applying for employment, a position or job, call it what you may, go to great lengths to present a carefully constructed currilicum vitae, a perfect covering letter, choose the appropriate clothing, gather as much information about the prospective employer for the job interview and are very happy when successful.

During the interview a salary or enumeration is negotiated by the prospective employer and employee to whom both parties agree.

But what do these words mean?

Let's go back to the dictionary!

Enumeration simply means "to count"- very important for budgeting.

Salary means "Fixed periodical payment." It can be called "Wages, Pay" or whatever. We shall not go into definition detail.

With other words enumeration or salary simply is what your employer will give you in return for your labour and or services.

The higher paid earners today not only negotiate payment but refined it to a payment, salary or enumeration package. This is very important as everybody must under all circumstances negotiate a "package" which at payday gives them the best monetary value for both the present and for the future!

Take special note that if you are employed on a contract or consulting basis the chances are very slim that your employer will offer you a package, thus you must make a thorough study of the position and make sure your payment rate value is negotiated so that it makes provision for covering all your needs and privileges so that you are not losing out in relation to your permanent employed and salaried counterparts.

What does a package consist of?

Usually it contains a basic salary plus fringe benefits (Perks).

- A basic salary is the money which will be paid out to you at the end of the month, week or other period negotiated.

- Yearly, holiday bonus or 13th cheque.

- A pension fund contribution of which is partly paid by the employer and partly by you and which in most countries are compulsory by law. (deducted from your salary per payment period)

- Group accident life and disability insurance.

- A medical fund contribution of which is partly paid by the employer and partly by you and which in most countries are compulsory by law. (deducted from your salary per payment period)

- Sick leave which in most countries are compulsory by law.

- Leave, holiday provision which in most countries are compulsory by law.

- A travel allowance or a company car.

- An entertainment allowance.

- A housing subsidy.

- A clothing allowance.

Make sure that there are no surprises when you receive your first payment advice or pay cheque, you must familiarize yourself with the contents of your employment contract, ensure that you have a copy of the contract, read it, investigate it as to ensure that you agree and accept it before you sign the contract and accept the position.

For the purpose of this book I shall stop here and not discuss packages which include company shares, profit sharing and so forth.

How should one construct the package which is negotiated with the new employer and be acceptable to both parties?

Here are a few pointers of what one should carefully consider.

The first step to take is, even before the interview, be sure to check with the tax offices/ internal revenue services of what the taxable scales on your basic salary will be and which of your **fringe benefits in the package are taxable or tax deductible**. Better still is to check and investigate your self and then call on an accountant, tax lawyer or both.

If you are presently employed test your present salary package and renegotiate with your employer. In most cases where you are an asset to you company they will consider reasonable improvements in reconstructing of your package.

<u>Salary.</u>

It is very important to know what you are worth to your prospective employer before you negotiate your salary package!

There are various methods of how to do a calculated estimate of what you are worth. Talk to personnel consultants, compare your educational levels, experience and other assets with that of positions in the employment columns of your newspapers, talk to human recourses managers of different companies, make use of the internet, use every possible tool available to you to ensure that you calculate your worth so that you are in a position

to:

a) Apply for a position where you do not price yourself out of the position, or

b) Where the employer see you coming and employ you at the lowest salary level as to ensure the maximum profit for himself.

Remember it is a fact that you will be judged on your previous salary/enumeration when you change employment.

To make sure that there are no surprises when you receive your first payment advice or pay cheque you must familiarize yourself with the contents of your employment contract, ensure that you have a copy of the contract, read it, investigate it as to ensure that you agree and accept it.

- Remember for budgeting purposes use your net or after deductions salary.
- Naturally we all negotiate for the highest basic salary. Make sure that the higher salary do not put you in a to high tax bracket, then rather go for a lower basic but negotiate a better housing subsidy deal or the best is to keep the high salary but make the correct pension fund adjustments as to offset the tax bracket.
- Negotiate with your employer or prospective employer to arrange a bigger contribution to your pension fund! Over 20 or 30years you will save hundreds of thousand if not millions of Rand through the extra saving, employer contribution and tax deductions.
- **Do not include salary increases into your budget until the day that your payment advice/pay slip have proof that it is actually paid out!**

Why:

- Very few employees if any know in advance how much the yearly increases will be.
- Employers will only know after their yearly salary review/assessment and board meetings of what percentage salary increases will be accepted can be afforded by the company or if there will be any salary increases at all.
- If you receive your increase letter, do not work that amount into your budget as there will be an increase of Tax, Pension Fund and other deductions.
- So, do not utilize or spend your increase before you know exactly how much **income or + money** it will be. If you're not careful with your increase the effect will be to utilize credit to balance your budgeted shortfall and that is fatal!
- Ask for advice from the trusty older generation in your family and most of all talk to you Bank Manager!
- The Bank Manager is surrounded by highly trained advisors whom will give you the correct advice simply because all banks need financially healthy customers which, without going into details, will keep his bank financially healthy! The banks will give this advice for free whereby independent financial advisors will ask a pot full of money.
- **Remember the old proverb "Do not count your chickens before they are hatched"?**

<u>Yearly, Holiday Bonus or 13th Cheque.</u>

Your holiday bonus must not be reflected in your budget as an income because most of the time it is already earmarked for your holiday, Christmas presents and various other necessities and your employers are not always under obligation to pay it out.

Some holiday bonuses and 13th cheques are linked to company profits and are therefore not always what you might have expected.

The best way to use your bonus is to immediately bank it in your savings account.

But Why?

- Remember earlier in the book I placed great emphasis on:
- Discipline to save and not waste.
- It will give you time <u>to think</u> about how best to use your bonus money.
- Budget out of your income for the holiday in the beginning of the year.
- By placing it in your savings account you naturally strengthen it, you will get a higher return on your interest which in turn will allow you to pay of your debt with the bank's money and or pay additional money into your home loan/bond, with the bank's money, and over the long term will save you a massive amount of money **<u>because of the money paid to You by the Bank.</u>**

It must be remembered that most bonuses are being paid out in November and early December of each year.

There are thousands of companies who want your bonus in there coffers!!

Ever wondered why the Christmas trees are already going up in stores by end of October, advertisements in every segment of the media increases between 200% and 300%, the banks relax there credit criteria and telemarketers from Life Insurance to toy companies phone you until you feel you are going to smash your telephone?

- It is very easy- they want to take your bonus for which you laboured for a very long year!!
- Ask for advice from the trusty older generation in your family and most of all talk to you Bank Manager!
- The Bank Manager is surrounded by highly trained advisors

whom will give you the correct advice simply because all banks need financially healthy customers which, without going into details, will keep his bank financially healthy! The banks will give this advice for free whereby independent financial advisors will ask a pot full of money.

Turn your penny twenty times and you will know how to spend your bonus or 13<u>th</u> cheque in the best way.

<u>**Your Pension Fund**</u>

<u>**Pension fund contribution of which is partly paid by the employer and partly by you and which in most countries are compulsory by law. (deducted from your salary per payment period)**</u>

How many of us realise or have realised the enormous importance of a pension fund!

If you haven't realised it the time is now to do just that.

Why?

- ## Retirement Comes In A Wink!!!

So Start To
Plan And Budget Immediately!

When you reach or come close to your retirement age it will be the most terrifying experience if you realize that, due to the cost and rapid rise in the cost of living, you are not in a financial position to retire or when being forced to retire by your company and not being able to cope financially. (Further attention to pension funds for self employed persons will be given in chapter 3.2 Expenditure. (Outflow of money)

Therefore great care must be taken with the caring, maintenance, understanding and how to budget for your pension fund.

<u>Here are a few pointers of making the most of your pension fund.</u>

- Make sure that there is a pension provision in your salary package!

If self employed, persons working on commission only, contract consultants, full time contractors, make sure you make ample provision for a pension fund or retirement annuity. Read the list under **<u>"Simple" chapter 1 again.</u>**

Further attention to pension funds for self employed persons will be given in chapter 3.2 Expenditure. (Outflow of money)

- Make sure that the pension fund is with a reputable financial institution! Get brochures, check on the internet and do everything possible to know more about your pension fund and what it will provide and not provide for you.
- Again-Because the pension portion of your salary isn't

taxable negotiate with your employer to increase your monthly pension contributions. In most countries your employer is obliged to pay the same amount as you pay towards <u>your</u> pension fund thus this will be a double plus to your pension fund which by your retirement will run into additional hundreds of thousands or even millions of R, $,Euro or whatever currency! Your employer will agree as there is a tax rebate for him as well as a happy employee. (Make 100% with your employer and Tax office of what the tax implications are)

- If you change employment, be retrenched or under what circumstances lose your job, do not spend your pension payout. Pay it into your next pension fund or pay of your house and increase your pension contributions when starting new employment. **You must keep your pension intact under all circumstances!**
- Do not borrow against your pension. Cut down on all nonessential commodities or expenditures but **keep your pension fund strong and healthy.**
- Make very sure what the taxation advantages and disadvantages are with your pension:
- What portion of your pension deducted from your salary is taxable?
- Is the pension portion taxable at all?
- What are the tax implications at retirement?
- What portion of your pension lump sum does your government tax and what portion is tax free?
- How much does your government tax the monthly or yearly pension payouts?
- It must be made very clear that in most countries there will be some sort of taxation. In South Africa pensions of all citizen's retirements will be taxed out of their wits.

But why then have a pension fund?

Because the financial advantages by far outstrips the disadvantages!

There are ways and means to offset taxation.

Get information from your local tax office.

Read all the tax relieve books supplied by your bank, insurance companies and Income tax offices.

If you are permanently employed and receive a salary the medical fund contributions will not be seen as an expenditure as for budgeting purposes you will only work with your net or after deductions salary as an income.

If you are self employed, working on commission, consulting or on contract and pay for this fund it will be seen as an expenditure.

- Ask for help from your pension fund manager and most of all talk to you Bank Manager!

The Bank Manager is surrounded by highly trained advisors whom will give you the correct advice simply because all banks need financially healthy customers which, without going into details, will keep his bank financially healthy! The banks will give this advice for free whereby independent financial advisors will ask a pot full of money.

Employment Group life, accident and disability insurance _of which is paid by the employer or partly by you and which in most countries are compulsory by law. (Deducted from your salary per payment period)_

This insurance is commonly known as on the job accident insurance and cover your life, limbs and ailments/medical conditions which is caused by conditions at your place of work.

To make sure that there are no surprises when you need to utilize/make use of your disability insurance, familiarize yourself with the contents of this contract, ensure that you have a copy of the contract, read and investigate as much as you can about the advantages of your insurance.

If you are permanently employed and receive a salary the contributions will not be seen as an expenditure as for budgeting purposes as you will only work with your net or after deductions salary as an income.

- If you are self employed, working on commission, consulting or on contract and pay for this fund it will be seen as expenditure. . (Make 100% with your employer and Tax office of what the tax implications are)

- Ask for advice from the trusty older generation in your family and most of all talk to you Bank Manager and disability Insurance Fund Manager!

<u>Medical fund contribution of which is paid by the employer or partly by you and which in most countries are compulsory by law. (deducted from your salary per payment period)</u>

Make very sure that you have a very good and trustworthy medical aid fund negotiated in your package. Make sure, and thoroughly investigate your medical fund, that the fund is reliable, not some fly by night and that you get your money's worth.

Due to the enormous cost of all medication, hospitalization, operations, medical tests and all medical care it is of the utmost importance to have a outstanding medical care fund.

Remember that in most countries a percentage of your medical care fund contributions are tax deductable which means that it is subsidised by the state and contribute to your savings!

There are a myriad of additional medical cover which can be bought through, mostly, the insurance companies but one must be wary that you do not double ensure and double pay for the same product which will not pay out if the one or the other pays out.

Make sure that you know the details of your medical fund contract so that you are sure that it is what you want and cover all you and your family's needs. With other words understand what it covers and ensure that you know what is written in the small print.

At first you might think that a medical fund is just expenditure but with the phenomenal increase of medical costs you will decry the day when sickness sets in and there is no fund available!

If you are permanently employed and receive a salary the medical fund contributions will not be seen as an expenditure as for budgeting purposes you will only work with your net or after deductions salary as an income.

If you are self employed, working on commission, consulting or on contract and pay for this fund and or compensate with a retirement annuity it will be seen as expenditure.

When working on commission or on a contract basis you must at least allow an additional 6% on top of your basic working salary to compensate for loss of pension funding.

- Ask for advice from the trusty older generation in your family and most of all talk to you Bank Manager!
- The Bank Manager is surrounded by highly trained advisors whom will give you the correct advice simply because all

banks need financially healthy customers which, without going into details, will keep his bank financially healthy! The banks will give this advice for free whereby independent financial advisors will ask a pot full of money. . (Make 100% with your employer and Tax office of what the tax implications are)

Sick leave.

Sick leave is a very important aspect of your salary package and in most countries it is compulsory by law. Do not waste your sick leave because it might be very important when you least expect it but also do not abuse yourself by not utilizing it when it is necessary. A great part of your financial independent success depends on your heath so use all the healthcare tools to your advantage as to ensure that you are healthy for as long as possible and to make money for as long as possible.

In some countries sick leave is compulsory even when working on a commission or contract basis. It will be very wise to study the laws of your country to determine of how to best structure your salary package.

When working on commission or on a contract basis you must at least allow an additional 6% on top of your basic working salary to compensate for loss of income during illness.

Insurance as an income protector can be bought from most insurance companies but very good care must be taken to ensure that you get value for money and that the small print is clear and understood.

It is, for obvious reasons, that women must negotiate proper maternity sick leave for themselves.

Again, know what the law/s of your country enforce on your employer and make sure that maternity leave is clearly stipulated in your contract of employment before you accept and sign it!

Leave, holiday provision.

It has been proven that, in this highly stressed and competitive working world in which modern man and woman inevitably finds them self's, time must be made to get away from it all and to give yourselves time to relax at home or away.

In most countries annual leave is compulsory.

Contract employed people and consultants usually do not have the privilege of compulsory annual leave, thus provision in your salary package must be made so that you have enough money to take an annual leave.

Study and find out of what the laws of your country provide for annual leave and or tax breaks.

Remember the adage that "All work and no play makes Tom a dull Boy"

It might just be said that "All work and no play will make Tom a sick, ineffective, uncompetitive and inefficient employee, individual and family man."

Most successful companies and businesses realises the importance of well treated employees.

Remember you must pay yourself even with breaks away from work and stress!

Travel/Car allowance and or a company car.

Automobile and or travel allowance is of great importance especially in South Africa and in other countries where most people travel great distances to work and or through long hours of traffic and where reliable public transport is non existent or inadequate.

Automobile prices, new or used in South Africa are very high thus a travelling allowance, car allowance or company car is a distinct advantage.

Usually these allowances give you the advantage of buying a vehicle and having a tax rebate! But care must be taken of what your country's Taxation Laws stipulate so that your vehicle or travel allowance does not become a financial burden rather than a monetary advantage.

- When negotiating your salary package enquire about how your new employer, or the present employer, can "structure" your salary or enumeration so as to give you the best tax advantage and subsequently the best monetary/financial advantage. More money to invest in you and your family's future.
- Make very sure of the tax implications when accepting a travel/car allowance and or a company car.
- When applying for a position try to gets it as close or within the shortest travelling time from your home as to maximize the effect of your car allowance and if you do not have an allowance it will maximize your savings on fuel/petrol and wear, tear and maintenance on your vehicle.

- Ask for advice from the trusty older generation in your family and most of all talk to you Bank Manager! (Make 100% with your employer and Tax office of what the tax implications are)
-
- The Bank Manager is surrounded by highly trained advisors whom will give you the correct advice simply because all banks need financially healthy customers which, without going into details, will keep his bank financially healthy! The banks will give this advice for free whereby independent financial advisors will ask a pot full of money.

Entertainment Allowance and Entertainment.

- If you are offered an entertainment allowance you must balance the high cost of entertaining, you and your family's feeling of regular entertaining other people, the position that you hold in the company with the tax deductibility /rebates, and value in your pocket that you can obtain from it. . (Make 100% with your employer and Tax office of what the tax implications are)

Make very sure of the tax implications when accepting an entertainment allowance.

With the high cost of entertainment and the fact that you start of by paying the high cost plus, in most countries, pay VAT (Value Added Tax) it is advisable to make sure of how to budget this allowance.

Ensure that if you have to do a lot of company related entertainment you are allowed to extent this privilege and have it increased if needed otherwise you end up paying for company expenses out of your own pocket.

Housing subsidy.

- Later in the book we shall discuss of how important a house, apartment, flat or any dwelling is in your retirement planning and saving. . (Make 100% sure with your employer and Tax office of what the tax implications are)

A housing subsidy is one of the most profitable fringe benefits that can be negotiated by you and if you do get one grab and hold on to it. The reasons is obvious:

- Your employer helps you to pay of one of, or the most important investments of your life;
- You will most probably be taxed on only a part of the subsidy;
- The subsidy amount which you do not have to pay can be saved with compound interest g until the savings amount is large enough to pay of your home or to buy a second dwelling;

<u>Clothing allowance.</u>

All allowances can be of great help to improve your overall monthly income as long as these are clearly to your monetary benefit.

- One must always ensure that whatever there is an allowance of this nature the value does not push you into a higher tax bracket and that if it does your country's tax system allow you to claim rebates. . (Make 100% with Tax office of what the tax implications are)

<u>3.1.2 Income from Small Business.</u>

I made a major mistake in underestimating the talents that the Good Lord gave me which I new I had from a very young age but never believed in, never utilized and worked with for my own and other's advantage.

If there is only one message that this book will convey to, be remembered by and put to use by the readers it is that nobody must underestimate the talents bestowed upon you!

Everybody do have one or more talents which you either know you have or you must discover- so discover it and or start working on it.

It is never to late to start exploring, investigating and using your talents.

Do not make the mistake that I made of only starting in my late fifties to write, use my talents as an artist, designing new products and patenting them.

Back to the small business!

For purposes of this book I shall not go into the detail of starting, developing, managing maintaining a small business but the reader must realise that the basics for a business stay the same as for your personal money generation namely that you must utilize every possible means of creating Income or **<u>Plus Money as to allow you to Save more.</u>**

<u>Thus Financial Planning, Proper Budgeting and clear headed management is just some of the same tools to be used as in your personal life!</u>

- Whether you have a talent or hobby use it to generate money but always start of with an investigative or test Budget. . (Make 100% sure with your Tax office of what the tax implications are)

The advantage of constructively using your talent/s or hobby/s as an small business is that you will enjoy it, it will not be as stressful as your main source of income and by following disciplined, basic business and personal principles it might just grow into the full blown business you always wanted or if so chosen keep it small but profitable for you and your family's needs at retirement.

Remember to always and meticulously Budget and to put your Profits into a Savings

Vehicle!

Do not resign from your employment at the first signs of success with your small business!!!

Remember:

- Your employer pays you a salary!
- Your employer pays part of your pension fund!
- Your employer pays part of your medical fund!
- Your employer pays part of your insurances, and fringe benefits e.t.c. e.t.c.!
- If you resign a reasonable position you will have to pay all of the above out of your own pocket and or out of your small business's profits!

Rather pay another trustworthy person to run the small business in your working time and control the essentials in your spare or hobby time. This will enable you to "learn the ropes" from a low risk position and determine whether and when the business can support you and your family's need and the need for a successful retirement!

Always make sure of your government assistance tools for small businesses.

- **You can, under certain conditions, run your small business from your own home, register your own home under the business's name and deduct the cost or part of the cost of the house from your income tax.** . (Make 100% sure with your Tax office of what the tax implications are)

<u>3.1.3 Income from Savings</u>

For the purpose of this chapter the definition for savings will be to have money in a savings account at a bank, building society post office or where ever.

To make sure that you pay yourself, the amount that you save each month in your savings account will be placed under the expenditure, minus money, section and the interest that you earn will be placed under income or plus money.

This is either an account where you can deposit money and withdraw whenever you like, a fixed deposit account or a savings plan account where money is deducted automatically per week or per month and be paid over into the savings account.

If you are in a position put money on a fixed account over a longer period my advice will be to not have the interest be paid out monthly but to let it accumulate within that account thus creating a compound interest situation.

The older people use to say "Let the bank pay interest on interest"

In South Africa we are fortunate to have savings rates at banks and other reputable savings institutions ranging from 5% to 12%.

The situation in Europe, the United States of America and for that matter the rest of the world is relatively low but so what, you get interest which is money that you do not have to work for, it discipline you to hoard money somewhere and most important of all it is a stepping stone to more lucrative investments such as a second property, South African Gold Kruger Rands or whatever.

Most financiers and financial advisors will say that to put money into a savings account is a loss and they are correct, because generally inflation, the periodic increase in prices of goods and or services, outstrips the interest rate which most banks pay. In South Africa, everybody having savings in a savings account gets taxed on the interest paid by the bank to you. But the tax on savings can be offset by tax rebates when filing your income tax returns and the end of the financial year-more detail on this subject in the chapter on taxation.

The secret here is then:

Not to use your savings or the interest thereof to pay for things you do not need and which is inflationary. Limit your personal inflation rate increases by staying out of the hyper inflation situation by not spending on high cost housing, expensive motor vehicles, brand name clothing, expensive food stuffs, take away meals, expensive restaurants, expensive furniture.

The interest on your savings increases your Income, Taxable Income and therefore the amount that you must pay tax. But who cares? Remember that most of your tax deductibles are calculated as a percentage on your taxable income so just make sure that you have a sound retirement annuity, medical fund and other tax deductibles. Although the percentage deductible stays the same, the amount of money increases because the percentage is calculated on a larger taxable income.

Do not under estimate the power of compound interest!!!!!

When Albert. Einstein was asked at one of his scientific seminars what power he considered the greatest in the universe, he answered, "The power of compound interest on your money in the bank!"

The simple market rule out there is supply and demand- so the more unnecessary junk you buy the more junk will be produced and the more the prices will be increased!

But why then do I in this book emphasise the importance of a solid savings account?

Remember that money in a savings account draws interest and the bank or building society **pays you money.**

Money kept long enough in a savings account and is increased every week or month from an early age, draws compound interest and the bank or building society **pays you more and more money.**

Cash in the bank allows you the power to negotiate a better deal when you buy property e.g. a bigger deposit gives you a smaller monthly payment or to swing it around you can use the interest on your savings to pay the monthly instalment.

If you own a house in South Africa and use your interest on your savings and pay it additionally into your bond account you get 6.5% compound interest on the savings and 10.5% compounded on your house bond. Even if the 6.5% interest on the savings interest being paid over is relatively small it will save you hundreds of thousands of rand if not millions of rand over twenty or even more over fifteen years because the 6.5% helps to reduce a 10.5% bond loan!

Your house in itself is a savings vehicle and generally increase in value by between 10% and 15%. So am I wrong in saying that by using your saving account smartly you can earn between 27.5% and 32.5% with a very low risk investment and save hundreds of thousands of rand over years on your bond?

Try your utmost to let the financial institutions pay you and that you use that payment to your greatest advantage.

Make a study of all interest paid by as many savings accounts, ordinary savings accounts, fixed deposit accounts, weekly, monthly fixed payment savings plans at various strong reliable banking and building society institutions to get the best interest on your money. Avoid the get rich quick schemes like a pest.

The amount of savings in whatever form you have will determine to what extent you have money freedom. The lack of savings in any form will simply complicate your life in all its aspects and make your future very complicated and very stressful.

The most power full aspect of a very strong savings account is that you have the assurance that you have Money!!

Money in the Bank is a stress reliever!!

It must be noted that many countries in Europe and in the USA are on a zero banking interest base. So savings in a bank is not profitable but if you have money in a bank you do have collateral, it forces you to accumulate money so as to make a loan to buy some profitable entity such as property, start your own small business, buy gold and silver and or gold and silver coins and so forth.

No money is an ultra stress builder!!

3.1.4 Income from Pension Fund

For the purposes of this book, only monies received/paid out from or by a pension fund, provident fund, retirement annuity fund or any other retirement vehicle to you the reader will be seen as income or Plus Money. For example, if you have already retired you will receive a pension/retirement annuity pay out, in what ever form.

For those who are not retired the payments that you are making towards a retirement provision vehicle, although it is a saving for your retirement, will be shown as expenditure in your budget because it is part of the money that you need to pay weekly, monthly or yearly and of paying yourself. You are your most important creditor but you must still pay and paying means expenditure or – money!

<u>Receiving Your Retirement Pension/Provident payout.</u>

<u>At retirement.</u>

Usually the payout of these retirement pensions is in the form of a lump sum or a lump sum and a monthly pension pay out.

Usually, especially in the event that you were employed by a government agency, you will be paid out a lump sum and a life long monthly pension.

Most private companies pay out a lump sum without the monthly pension pay outs.

At pay out make very sure you know that your pension is paid into a reliable low risk savings vehicle!

My advice is to have your retirement money paid into a fixed savings account for a minimum period of three months as to allow you a "Cool Of Time" to study and carefully consider you many options. The best attribute of this option is that the bank or building society must pay you interest while you study and consider your options!!!

Do not immediately pay your hard earned money over into an annuity!

Do not immediately pay your hard earned money over into a property development scheme.

Do not immediately pay your hard earned money over to a financial advisor to invest into investment portfolios of which you do not know much or anything and ten to one he also does not know!

Do not ever pay your hard earned money over into any "Get Rich Quick Scheme" because these just don't exist!!!

Do not immediately pay your hard earned money over to your children, remember one of the most important messages of this book is that there is a very good chance that:

- You might live longer than you expected;
- The cost of living is going, continuously, to increase;
- If you do not have sufficient "other income or + money" the day to day costs of survival will become more and more expensive.
- Do not buy a yacht, speed boat, flashy automobile or any "dream retirement" vision because you are immediately going to lose money through depreciation.
- Do not go and gamble with your money simply because millions of people are continuously losing their money. To put it bluntly the casinos, horse racing industry, Bingo operators, and Lotto operators must take your money firstly to cover their running costs, pay their share holders and taxes. Gamble isn't a high monetary risk it is a certain monetary risk!
- The taxation liabilities and your tax deductibles must be studied in depth before making your retirement money investment decisions.
- My advice is to have your retirement money paid into a fixed savings account for a minimum period of three months as to allow you a "Cool Of Time" to study and carefully consider you many options. The best attribute of

this option is that the bank or building society must pay you interest while you study and consider your options!!!

The same principals will apply for retirement annuities, long term retirement savings plans or any retirement savings vehicles.

The pros and cons of various retirement plans and some advice of how best to invest the proceeds from these will be discussed in more detail in the

<u>Expenditure or Minus Money chapters.</u>

<u>3.1.5 Inheritance.</u>

How many persons have inherited a substantial estate but only got a fraction of that inheritance's value?

Due to the fact that most inheritances are brought about by the death of a dear family member the following happens.

The family member dies.

This is a very traumatic period for the family.

Most of the family is so traumatised that they are in a state of not thinking clearly.

All the organization for funeral arrangements, informing distant family, friends, business associates and colleagues just aggravates the situation.

Some of the family are so obsessed with the inheritance that they, in some cases, and in a frenzy, grab and get hold of the deceased's will and immediately start discussing it with the rest of the family, appoint a executor or agent on behalf of the executor who usually very quickly <u>initiates</u> the execution of the estate. The estate executor/agent usually are very quick to start the administration of the deceased estate but not so quick to finalise the execution of the estate. But why? Through the prolonged administration they make money by receiving interest on the estate(you and your family's money), by having more time to bill higher executioner's fees/costs to their dispersements/service bill.,

Be very careful to thoroughly investigate the estate executor's fee beforehand, if not expressly specified in the will and or agent's aggrement before signing it.

Do not treat an inheritance irresponsibly!!

Why not?

You and your family, under these traumatized circumstances do not know the real value of the estate!

You and your family, under these traumatised circumstances do not know the real cost of estate execution!

Examples:

When my dear late mother died;

The duplex apartment that was sold out of the inheritance by me and my sister for R160, 000-00 was in three years time valued at

R500, 000-00.

What I am trying to convey to the reader is that:

There must be a cooling of period agreed to by you and your family as to:

Get over the trauma and shock;

Calmly discuss the execution of the estate;

Find out /investigate all the costs of execution of the estate;

Plan the execution of the estate;

Find out the real value of the estate!

Find out the <u>real future</u> value of the estate!

If the will does not expressly appoint an executor make sure you and your family appoint an appropriate executor or agent on behalf of the executor as so nominated. Rather appoint a family member or members as executors to work with your bank or building society.

My advice is to have your inheritance money as received from the estate paid into a fixed savings account for a minimum period of three months, as to allow you a "Cool Of Period" to study and carefully consider your options. The best attribute of this option is that the bank or building society must pay you interest while you study and consider your options!!!

Take good care of all other property as to preserve and maintain it until final calculated decisions can be made.

If a house, apartment or any other real estate is part of your inheritance do not just sell it after receiving it out of the estate!

Make sure what the value and future value is.

Make sure what the Renting/Letting value and future value is.

Make sure what the value and future value of developments in the area of the property is.

Make sure what the future value will be if maintenance is done and improvements and extensions are made to the property.

Make very sure of what the monetary effect will be if you or a family member occupy the home!

Ask for advice from the trusty older generation in your family and most of all talk to you Bank Manager!

The Bank Manager is surrounded by highly trained advisors whom will give you the correct advice simply because all banks need financially healthy customers which, without going into details, will keep his bank financially healthy! The banks will give this advice for free whereby independent financial advisors will ask a pot full of money.

The deceased worked, in some or another way, hard throughout his life to build his estate and now there is an obligation on you and your family to execute his last will in a caring and responsible way!

See Schedule 1 containing a brief and user friendly explanation of the administration process.

3.1.6 Income from Additional Property
Buying a First Property
Buying an Additional Property
House or other Dwelling.

In all of the developed world an income from an additional property or properties has become one of the best investments ever! With careful consideration and calculation the rental from a second, or more, home or other dwelling can pay the bond, maintain the property, bring in a healthy monthly income and will be a very profitable future investment.

Property is and will be, for a very long time, be a stable investment if thought through and calculated very carefully!

Remember that the world population is growing, this population must live somewhere.

Many of the under developed or so called third world countries are developing at an alarming pace.

Remember that the key to buying anything and especially home or other dwelling is money.

To have sufficient money you must have an income and or substantial savings of some sort.

The banks, building societies or any financial institution will not lend you, in simple terms, give you a bond if they do not have proof of your income which is only a nice way of telling you that they want proof that you have the means to pay them back plus interest at low risk to the lending or bond institution.

The cost of your home and additional property will be discussed in more detail dealing with the expenditure section of your budget.

3.1.7 In come from Shares on the Stock Market.

There are money to be made on the stock market but with the provision that you know what you are doing.

Make sure that you find a reputable stock market agent and if not totally sure of its integrity consult your bank manager or the bank's financial advisor

To start of, study share trading in any possible way, books, news paper article, short inexpensive study courses at a college or university, financial magasines or whatever or wherever you can get insight into and knowledge about the world of share trading.

Start with small affordable investment amounts until by trial and error and overall general insight gained, you can make larger money out of the stock market.

Remember to, as with everything else- Budget every income and Expenditure.

3.1.8 Valuables

My advice is that before you give away, sell or throw anything always ensure that you do not get rid of a valuable!

My personal feeling of a valuable is that it either has a sentimental, monetary value or both.

So before you get rid of anything have it evaluated and then make a proper decision of what to do.

There are various methods of evaluation and cross investigation available such as the internet, the pawn shops in the rich areas of your town or city, professional evaluators' and appraisers, jewel makers and jewel shops, art galleries and so forth.

Remember that if you get an evaluation from a pawn shop or dealer that you double the price of the evaluation as the pawn entrepreneurs will, as a rule, always only offer you fifty percent(50%) of the real value.

So at spring cleaning, garage or packing space clearing evaluate what you want to just dump.

The trend in South Africa today, when one's parents or other family member pass away, is to get a second hand dealer or pawn shop business to come and buy the "old stuff" that nobody wants!

These second hand dealers or pawn shop business owners buy at rock bottom prices and then make a fortune out of antiques, antique restoration, furniture restoration, jewellery, paintings and other valuables-just because the original owners wanted to get rid of everything as quick as possible and make a few quick bucks!

So before dumping anything get all persons who have an interest involved, do a preliminary valuation, and do an in-depth evaluation and then and only then sell at rock bottom or throw away.

3.1.9 Income from Taxation

Everybody in the developed, free, capitalist, communist, democratic world or whatever system the country is ruled by must and will pay some form of income tax.

In most countries tax is gathered by subtracting the tax deductions from and in accordance with your income, in whatever form it is earned.

What very few people realise is that in most countries there are some money to be made from your income tax that you have paid!

Part of the rich being rich is that they have accountants, tax lawyers and or tax advisors who retrieve massive amounts of money from the internal revenue services by means of tax deductibles, tax concessions and tax rebates which is within the tax laws of most countries. Most rich people make an effort to also know the tax laws and system in their particular country.

We diligently pay tax because of the obligation but, we the ordinary hard working people of the world, rarely exercise our right to claim back the tax deductibles which is ours by law, either through working to hard and not having time to study the tax system or through sheer ignorance!

If you want to save money Make time and do not be Ignorant!!!

Here are just a few of the items on which you can claim back a percentage of the Tax you paid, valid in most countries:

- Contributions to a retirement annuity;
- Contributions to a private Medical Fund;
- Levies on medical costs prescribed by a Medical Doctor but not paid by your medical fund;
- Rebates on you automobile; and
- If you work from home or run a business from home up to 25% of your bond payment or rent can be tax deductable to name but a few.

Millions of people who fall below the minimum yearly income bracket and who are not required by law to submit their yearly income tax submissions do not realize that:

Tax is still being deducted from their income/salaries (Pay As You Earn.);

Tax is still being deducted by means of VAT on every article which they buy. (Value Added Tax); and

- That Contributions to a retirement annuity;
- Contributions to a private Medical Fund;
- Levies on medical costs prescribed by a Medical Doctor but not paid by your medical fund; and
- Various other costs to yourself can be partially recovered from the tax system and within your country's tax laws.

The irony of the fact of not submitting an Income Tax form/submission is that you can not claim any deductions/rebates.

So:

If you earn less than R120,000-00 per annum (Minimum for being exempted to submit a tax assessment in South Africa) and pay for a retirement annuity, or any retirement fund, pay for a medical fund e.t.c. submit your tax assessment and claim the deductions that you are entitled to by law.

Persons in other countries must study their tax laws to ensure that they get the maximum benefit from these rebates!

If you cannot afford an accountant, tax lawyer or tax advisor to get the maximum benefit from tax deductibles then:

- Get as much information from your nearest Tax/ revenue office.
- Get, Read and Study all the brochures, booklets and other information/ material that is supplied by your Tax/ Revenue office.
- Study your tax assessment and the instruction booklet that comes with it.
- Make use of the internet, most country's tax/ revenue departments have websites where valuable information can be retrieved.
- Talk to your bank manager, most banks have tax advisors who will give you free tax advice because they know that the money that you recover will be deposited into your bank account.
- Study tax law. If you have the means and have the time, do a diploma or degree in tax law. Various colleges and universities have short intense courses in tax law.

It will give you a proper insight into your obligations and rights of your country's tax laws, save you a lot of money, give you the chance of practicing as an tax advisor and give you that added advantage of adding an additional qualification to your CV.

- Read as many published books on the subject of taxation

as possible, there are many very informative books in the book stores, libraries and on the internet.

- For South Africans I shall strongly recommend the life assurance company Old Mutual's book "Old Mutual Income Tax Guide" published by Butterworth's and translated into my home language, Afrikaans, as "Ou Mutual Inkomste Belasting Gids"

<u>Future Income.</u>

Excluding future pay rises, bonuses investments of all sorts, the proper maintenance of all your present assets will be highly valuable in the future.

Remember prices of everything will rise!

Keep your present home in a good state of maintenance and in future you will get a better price for it, the same principal stand for your other assets.

Keep your automobile in good condition, the service book updated and you will be surprised at the good price you can get for it after driving it for six to eight years, you might even find that you got half the car for free.

<u>3.1.10 Profit</u>

Do everything you do for a profit.

With every thing that you do or buy think of how you can make a profit out of it.

Profit can also be in other forms than in money e.g.

If you want to see a movie at a cinema make sure it is a good movie that must be seen on the big screen. If there isn't good movies at the cinema rather take out a DVD/blueray. You will save money and the frustration of wasting money, time and spoiling an evening which should have been an enjoyable outing.

The reasonable average hamburger in South Africa costs R35.50. Buying fresh hamburger patties from the local butcher and the rest of the ingredients from the café next door I make a beautiful burger for R3.50!!

The Toyota Carrola which I maintained immaculately and used for five years I sold for more than the original selling price. I only lost the interest for the two years in which I paid the loan.

To close the chapters on Income or Plus Money I again want to stress that all legal means of saving money for your living, future life and retirement must be pursuit.

You do not have to be obsessed with money but we on this earth will have to make time to think about it because governments, countries, politicians, banks, other financial institutions your employers, family friends or nobody is not going to do it for you!

While you have an income one never really think of what this income provides for!

But once there is no income all of us very quickly and under massive stress realise that there are no MONEY to pay:

The home loan/ bond or rent;

Food;

Car/Automobile HP;

Clothing;

Telephone;

Water and electricity bills;

School fees; and

Other expenses.

It is an harrowing experience to try and juggle oneself out of the enormous pressure brought about by the banks, credit bureaus, telephone companies, postal companies,

and tens of other credit entities that are going to demand their payment at the end of the month. They will not care that you have a temporary problem of losing your job or a business setback, because they want their MONEY! You are now a risk to their income and no financial institution will tolerate the risk of losing their MONEY ! While you earn a reasonable income and have reasonable fixed assets all financial institutions will give you maximum credit and to the maximum limits but as soon as you do not have enough monthly Income to, at least, cover your monthly Expenditure you are a risk. All your assets, house, cars/automobiles furniture and every other asset is seen as only collateral in case they have to liquidate you as a means to recover their MONEY. All these institutions will not give you a loan to survive, renovate your house to realize a better selling price because you already are a risk with one set of Expenditure and they will not, in the least and under no circumstance, go into a double risk situation.

Above all, remember the maxim" All work and no play will make Tom a dull boy" But do it responsibly!

Chapter 4

4 <u>Expenditure. (Outflow of Money or Minus, Money)</u>

<u>4.1 Life Essentials</u>

Introduction.

4.1.1 Cost of Food

4.1.2 Cost of Housing

4.1.3 Cost of Transport

4.1.4 Cost of Clothing

4.1.5 Cost of Medical Aid

4.1.6 Cost of Insurance.

4.1.7 Cost of Children

4.1.8 Cost of Banking Savings

4.1.9 Cost of Investments

4.1.10 Cost of Shares(Stock Market)

4.1.11 Cost of Taxation

4.1.12 Cost of Non essentials

<u>4.1 Life Essentials</u>

<u>Introduction.</u>

We all know that you cannot buy anything unless we have money to do so and that this buying experience is nothing else than an expenditure.

Long gone are the days when we inherited farms, or somewhere just got a piece of land to farm.

Long gone are the days where we could use rock, clay, wood or any building material for free from nature to build a house.

Long gone are the days where we could all plant, raise livestock, hunt or gather

from nature to satisfy our food requirements.

We cannot get transport, clothes and all of life's essentials without buying it and for that buying we need money!

All land today belongs to somebody, either it belongs to the government, companies or other individuals and if we want it we somehow have to buy it!

So does everything else that we need and want.

The world is ruled by supply and demand and whether you want to supply or demand you need money to do it.

Through demand and increased demand, prices of all commodities rise due to higher supply costs and profit taking. The demand side of life isn't ruled just by essentials but also a demand for more luxuries, easier lifestyles, brand names, gizmos like sell/mobile phones, expensive toys, better education more expensive vacations and a host of new life essentials.

The population growth and the better and higher lifestyle expectations of this growing population is increasing demand all over the world and subsequently

price increases will accelerate.

Due to computerisation, automation, advanced technology fewer and fewer unskilled and semi skilled labour will be needed.

But what am I trying to do, scare the reader?

No I am not trying to scare anybody but between the normal trials and tribulations of life, growing populations which will bring greater job/profession competition, rapid cost of living increases, retrenchments, lay offs, restructuring, job losses due to technology and automation advances, spiralling profit demands and most of all more people living longer with fewer government resources to assist the elderly I strongly want to sensitise as many people to think, plan and budget their monetary future as to survive financially.

Seventeen years ago I lost my wife due to cancer and over and above the massive grievance which me and my two children had to overcome we also lost, to be earthly about it, her salary as part of the house hold income and above all her expertise of buying food.

Seven years ago the company by whom I was employed for twelve years was, under very suspicious conditions, "liquidated".

I am quite well educated and qualified but due to my relative advanced age

I could only find contract work for short periods of the year and my salaried income were reduced to one third of my usual yearly income.

What pulled me through?

I, although always thrifty and careful with the use of money, was forced to think, calculate plan and budget as to allow our family to survive!!!!!

A good friend of mine once said. "Always live every day as if it is your last day but budget and save money for just in case you live tomorrow."

Please note that as with the Income or PLUS Money chapters, the sub chapters

For Expenditure or MINUS Money will correlate with the budget subsections in your budget CD and budget forms as to allow quick reference with the book itself.

The bottom line of saving money is to ensure that you do not spend more than what you budgeted for. With other words your expenditure must be less than your income and then and only then do you have money to save!

4.1.1 <u>Cost of Food/Groceries.</u>

The one aspect of life with which nobody can go without is food and that is why I chose it as the first expenditure.

But what is there to say about food accept that we must eat?

Do the following even before you start your food/grocery section of your budget:

- Look at your fruit and vegetable rack and see how many items you paid for which went "off", is rotten and not fit for digestion;
- Look into your refrigerator and see how many items you paid for which went "off", is rotten and not fit for digestion and which you will throw into the dust/disposal bin;
- Look at your freezer and see how many items, meat, frozen vegetables and fish you paid for is still lying there for weeks and sometimes months;
- Look at your grocery cupboards and see how many items you paid for, which you haven't used or do not use that often but because it is on your standard grocery list, physically or mentally, you buy over and over out of habit;
- Look at your bathroom cupboards and cabinets and see how many items you paid for which is heaping up. Half and three quarters bottles of shampoo, conditioners, disinfectants, toothpaste tubes and many other items which must and can still be used;
- Go and look in your laundry and garage and you might just find a huge amount of useable items for which you will have to pay to buy again; and
- Take time go and sit and think of your buying patterns, of the wastage in your home.

Remember that everything which you buy is turning income or Plus money into expenditure or Minus money. All the items standing around and which is eventually thrown away is money that, if left in your savings account would have generated interest and turned into income and more Plus money. If you paid for these items with your credit card this will even be worse because now you throw away items for which you paid with money you did not have and upon which you pay very high interest.

Plan and budget your food/grocery purchases so as not to waste.

Use what is available in your home first before wasting money by buying of what you already have.

Do not travel long distances to buy so called bargains and specials because:

Fuel is expensive

The advertiser of the bargain or special usually increase the price of all the other items in his store

If the special is at worthwhile price make sure you and your family needs it, will use it and then buy enough.

Work on the trolley cost of the same item list when comparing best price wholesalers and stores.

Do not buy anything you or your family does not NEED or cannot AFFORD!

One must also be aware of items which have a sudden and steep increase in price.

Doing my monthly grocery shopping for the month of March at my supermarket and scanning the chocolate rack for my monthly treat, I noticed, on a quick calculation, that the price increased by fifteen percent (15%) per slab from the previous month.

As I was still contemplating this massive increase a young lady and her daughter arrived and looking at the chocolate the lady remarked, " Look at that price – no chocolate this month and before you complain, we won't die going without it."

It was at that moment that I decided that I shall not overpay 15% for my chocolate and that I to can go without it.

To my astonishment the same and other brands of chocolate dropped by 18% in July, only three months later-but why?

Very simple, the sales of chocolate dropped, a lot of chocolate lovers realized the price is too high and stopped buying and that they "Will Not Die" going without it.

Inflation, basically, means "Price Rises" or it can be described as the rate or ratio by which prices of various items increases over certain time periods.

Now there are many aspects that drive this so called inflation namely an increase in the cost of:

Production;

Raw Materials;

Labour; and

Distribution and Delivery to name but a few inflationary contributors.

In South Africa the price of petrol/diesel/fuel or, as the Americans call it – gasoline" is one of the main inflation/price rise contributors. Every time the petrol price is increased all prices goes up within two months.

What "Boggles'" my mind is that the price of petrol rise with 4 % and within two months the price of everything rise with 4%. What the average person in the street does not realise is that the suppliers of everything and especially foodstuffs use, or rather misuse, the fuel price rise and other price rises to simply push up the price of their of their products to a point which is totally out of proportion.

Let me give an example . If a truck transported 10,000 slabs of chocolate to its destination the transport cost rises with 4% after the fuel price hike and then suddenly the price of chocolate rises with 4%. This is totally untrue because the total fuel price rises with 4% but the supplier/manufacturer delivers 10,000 slabs of chocolate! Thus the price rise of an R 19.00 slab of chocolate cannot rise by 4% but by 4% divided by 10,000 and thus only by 0.0004%.

When the price of foodstuffs which we cannot go without, like for instance bread, raise with ridiculous percentages-then bake your own bread or find an alternative.

This world of ours is ruled by supply and demand and if the demand keeps rising prices will increase. If the demand for any commodity drops due to the public not essentially needing it and stop buying it the manufacture will have no choice but to lower its prices or go bankrupt.

To shield our selves against this so called INFLATION is to limit ourselves to the negative influence of INFLATION.

Save money by not buying non essentials, save money so that the banks pay YOU interest, save money so that you can invest some of that interest returns into areas where you make more money than the interest that the bank pays and to offset inflation where you just cannot avoid the impact of inflation.

4.1.2 Cost of Housing

All of us need a place to live and thus to have a proper "roof over our heads".

Buying or renting a home can be a very expensive undertaking and must be thoroughly thought through-whether it is a house, duplex, flat or any other dwelling.

My farther always said and I quote "A wife, a house, and a car, a horse-think very carefully before getting it on your name, because if you don't the money implications will start once it is in your name"-unquote.

It is more profitable to buy rather than rent but if you cannot afford to buy, rent in such a manner as to allow yourself to save for a decent deposit on a house.

Another probable route to follow if you do not have the means to buy a house is to go into a "Hire Purchase Agreement".

This is a contractual agreement whereby the intention of the buyer and seller is that the buyer will lease the dwelling over a certain period of time at a certain price and then have the option of buying the property with the past payments being accepted as a downpayments on this property.

Before deciding on this method of property acquisition I very strongly advise to obtain sound legal advice and have this legal advice confirmed by the financial institution through which you intend to apply for the eventual bond.

The reason for my concern simply is that the laws governing this form of purchasing contract are very complicated in most modern countries.

Save money at the bank or other financial institution through which you intend buying the house/dwelling. This saving will enhance your chances of getting a bond or other means of financing your home because you already have a record at this institution which will strengthen your credit rating. The interest earned on your savings will help build your savings account and pay, fully or partly, for your bond after it has been approved and registered.

When buying a property, and for that matter anything you buy on a bond, loan, vehicle finance or any form of buying on credit, it must clearly be known that there are major aspects that will impact on your monetary status namely:

i) You have to pay monthly instalments to cover the capital sum. (Payback time for the Bond/Loan)

ii) You have to pay monthly instalments to cover the interest on that capital sum. (Payback time for the interest on the Bond/Loan)

iii) This bond will influence your monthly and yearly budget.

iv) Ensure you know what the interest rate on the sale is and make provision for governmental interest rate hikes/increases. If and when the interest rate drops adjust your budget but put the gain in a savings vehicle as to save for the next interest rate increase-which at some stage will materialise.

Cognisance must be taken of various costs even before any property can bought, e.g.

The purchase price of the house.

Initiation Costs

Security Evaluation Costs.

Property Transfer Costs (Transfer Lawyers)

Bank/Loan Institution Bond Costs

Bank/Loan Institution Bond Lawyers Costs. Ensure that the title deed is in the seller's name and that what restrictions there are, such as servitudes and other restrictions.

Registration of Title Deed

Registration of Home Bond

Local government authority/municipality Rates and Taxes.

Local government authority/municipality water and electricity costs.

Make one hundred percent sure that the local government authority/municipality's water, electricity, rates and tax outstanding amounts/invoices has been paid up by the previous owner.

The seller, property agency nor the bond financial institution will check this aspect for you.

If there is an outstanding amount on the municipal accounts demand that the previous owner pay it or demand an equal reduction in selling price before you sign any documents which will finalise the purchase!

If not you might find yourself with a massive outstanding expense, no water and or electricity!

Make sure that you buy the home/house building plan/s from your local government authority/municipality and then make sure that you know if there are any illegal additions and take the necessary steps to ensure that the seller update the plans.

Make sure from the plan/s to where all the sewage, water drainage, water piping and electricity cabling are laid as this can be a hazard when doing your own extensions and improvements.

I had the bad experience when installing a swimming pool and found that the water drainage pipe ran slap dash through the one corner of the pool when the hole digging was in process. The outcome of this was that I had to change the house plan, get a plumber to reroute the piping which, in both instances, cost me money and delayed the project for a full month

A percentage of minimum 5% must be added on top of the selling price of the house in your budget when planning to buy.

So before you apply for the bond do a dummy budget BEFORE you apply for the bond and calculate what the influences will be on your monetary capabilities.

Most banks and financial institutions have bond calculators on their web sites which allow you to see in advance what the costs will be.

Better still go to the bank and let them give you a quotation.

Always shop around for the best deal but make sure that you only use reputable institutions.

As a priority it must be known that the interest component on a bond is the major part of the money you will spend on that house or other home. Over a thirty or forty year loan period you will pay, interest alone, at a sum of approximately 3 times of what that house originally cost! Example:

The interest on a home in South Africa bought for an initial R 900,000-00 at an annual interest rate of 10.5% over 20years will be approximately R3,000,000-00 and NOT including bank administration and other costs!

So how can you defeat this interest monster?

It is very easy –pay back the bond as quickly as possible by additional payments. See what the interest on your savings are, pay the same amount or more, what ever you can afford, extra into your savings account and let your savings account grow for six(6) months then pay a lump sum from your savings of on the bond!

Make sure with your bond institution that the loan amounts and interest are recalculated and adjusted!

Keep enough in your savings account for a rainy day and or a bit more interest payment from the bank.

You will be amazed to see how quickly the bond sum shrinks if this or the same type of approach is followed –pay the bank's interest of with the interest they pay you and more!

Buy as little as you can on credit as you must pay interest on that credit, but where you do have a credit account make sure that it is within your budget and that, and this is essential, you pay it regularly.

Why? Simply because a credit account kept under proper control and managed in a responsible manner will also work to your advantage when applying for a home loan/bond because the financial institutions will check your general credit rating and a well managed credit account will increase your credit rating which is to your advantage.

Banks are, generally, very wary of risk loans as this poses a financial risk to the bank and they will not approve your bond or loan application if your risk profile shows that you are not able to regularly and constantly pay back the loan. The financial institutions will do a risk analysis and profile on you-so through proper budgeting you can create a low risk profile from a very early stage in your life.

Although I discussed housing in the expenditure section of this book as an expenditure I shall definitely categorise it as a "Positive

Expenditure" because, if maintained and managed correctly, it will be an asset and a savings vehicle. It can be sold at a profit

The more capital and interest you pay back the bigger your profit will be when selling the home.

If you decide not to sell at an early stage and pay the bond of quicker the earlier you can live in that house for free and that will set the total bond payments free to be saved for your retirement.

4.1.3 Cost of Transport

A Car/Automobile or Any Vehicle.

If you have a good public transport system why buy a car?

If on a rainy day you desperately need a car –Hire one for the day!

Vehicle Prices Has Sky Rocketed Beyond Reason and Logic !

As with all credit buying or otherwise stated, buying with any form of a loan, buying a vehicle have a capital and interest payback structure. The only difference is that the interest rate is usually higher on vehicle financing.

I could never figure out why this interest rate must be higher than that on a home bond. I asked a bank manager - he had a long and non understandable explanation of what the reason/s was and that is mainly because vehicle financing is considered a short term loan.

My personal and only explanation is that with a home bond there is a much longer period over which to maximise interest and profit and that vehicle finance is a greater risk to financial institutions than that of a home loan or bond.

A very distinctive difference between buying a vehicle and buying a home is that the moment that the vehicle is registered in your name it starts to lose value!

When buying a new vehicle it loses ten percent (10%) of its value when you drive it out of the dealer's show rooms! Thus buying a vehicle/car/automobile is a very good example or definition of "Depreciation" OF AN ITEM OR MONEY!

When buying a second hand car, or nowadays called a previous owned car (called so to disguise the fact that it is second hand or used) the situation is the same as for buying a new vehicle except for the fact that you will not get the same warranty, you do not know how the previous owner treated this car and what unknown and hidden defects are in this vehicle-whatever the situation you will be forced to pay back the loan and With INTEREST!

Do not Ever compete with the Joneses, it is fatal, because as previously stated you just do not know if the Joneses are Rich, have a greater Income than yours, make money through Criminal activity or is on the brink of bankruptcy!

When buying a vehicle ensure that it is affordable, both in the purchase price and after sales maintenance e.g. the servicing costs of this vehicle.

A vehicle if managed correctly can become a valuable asset and can contribute, at a later stage, to your income or Plus money, for example:

i) I bought a new Toyota Carrola in 1989 for 36,000 South African Rand (Approximately 30,000 US Dollar in those days) , paid off extra on my monthly instalments which resulted in paying a three year contract of in eighteen months and saving a massive amount on loan interest which I did not have to pay over the full term.

ii) Then by making sure that I properly maintained this car and ensuring that the service logbook is kept up to date by the dealer after servicing, I drove this vehicle for a further five years and 87,000 kilometers or 54,000 miles.

iii) I sold this vehicle to the mechanic who always serviced it at the vehicle agency from which I bough the car for 20,000 South African Rand.(Approximately 17,000 US Dollar).

So what am I trying to say? – You can save money when buying a vehicle.

But what did I actually SAVE?

a) By paying extra I saved eighteen months of interest which would have gone into the pockets of the financial institution-that saving I paid into my special savings account on which the financial institution paid me interest!

b) I drove a car for free for five years which gave me the freedom of saving the total loan payment, pay it into my special savings account - on which the financial institution paid me interest!

c) By maintaining the car properly I sold it for a "sort of a profit" which in turn gave me a large enough amount for a deposit/down payment on a new car. This deposit was large enough to again cut the total loan amount so as to limit the monthly payments and lower the INTEREST on the loan and interest payment period.

I shall always recommend buying a new vehicle, as long as it is affordable and from a reputable manufacturer. The reason is that with a new vehicle you will have a better guarantee/warranty, the first person, you, driving this vehicle will care for it and if sensible maintain it carefully.

If a new vehicle is not affordable and you must buy a previous owned/used/second hand one, then make sure of the following:

i) Make sure that the service record is available-the service log book so as to ascertain whether the previous owner maintained this vehicle to the manufacturers specifications.

ii) Take note of the mileage on the odometer and that the reading corresponds with that of the service record. The higher the mileage the less you pay for it.

iii) Shop around for the best deal and the most reputable dealer.

iv) Talk to your bank/financial institution because most reputable banks/ financial institutions has preference and accredited vehicle agencies with whom they prefer to do business with and will then give loans easier to prospective clients.

v) Make sure that the vehicle have a roadworthy certificate from the government or local government authority.

vi) Make sure that the warranty or guarantee is available to you and in your purchasing contract and if not fully satisfied or understandable let an attorney/ lawyer read and analyse it for you.

vii) Make sure with your local police and traffic departments that this vehicle isn't stolen as this will have dire consequences if the vehicle is traced by the vehicle theft department of the police.

viii) Inspect and double check the overall condition of the vehicle. Special note must taken of the condition of the paint work, upholstery, oil and water leaks, smooth running of the engine, smooth gear changing, presence of RUST e.t.c., e.t.c.

vii) Test drive the vehicle to ensure that it travel and drive to your satisfaction.

If you buy a second hand vehicle which isn't up to scratch it will, in a very short period cost you more than a new vehicle and create a massive expenditure and Minus money which in turn will impact negatively on your budget.

Whether buying a new or previously owned vehicle make sure that it is affordable, of a reliable manufacturer, has a proper warrantee/guarantee, that the service and maintenance of the vehicle is affordable and that it is value ensured.

4.1.4 Cost of Clothing

If not managed wisely clothing can be a major drainage of money and a great negative influence on your budget. (Minus Money)

It is a given that everybody must be clothed and that everybody wants to be smart and neatly clothed-which is natural and proper but, again, do not compete with the Joneses!

The three main culprits in buying clothing are possibly-Buying the so called "Brand Names", buying it at the so called "Elite Shops" and to complete the disaster "Buying this clothing on Credit".

By buying clothing on credit you will be paying an interest rate higher than that which your financial institution pays you on your savings, what they charge interest on your home bond or on your vehicle financing!

If you are not rich do not buy the so called "Brand Names", do not buy at the so called "Elite Shops" and do not participate in the disaster of "Buying these clothing on Credit".

At one stage me and my wife also fell into the trap of buying clothing on credit until one day, and by accident, we took notice of what was on the monthly statement-and what did we find on analysing it:-

The "Brand Name" clothing cost three to four times what the same quality and design of the non "Brand Names" cost!

We paid 21% interest on this credit- which is not a credit but loan, a liability and treble the interest that we get on our savings account!

We were billed an amount that calculated to 5% of the purchases for so called club membership on which we also paid interest. What did we get for this club membership? We got a booklet full of advertisements on a monthly basis, which I always threw in the dust bin before my wife or daughter could see it – so we were paying for the chain store's ADVERTISEMENTS!

A one stage I discussed this "Club Membership" with my wife and we decided to cancel it and then saved a bit of money

Shop around and think before you just buy.

Men, women and children can and will want brand name or good quality clothing, but limit these for Saturday, Sunday and special occasions and do not buy these on credit. Why in heavens name do you want to wear a brand name garment when going to buy groceries, work in the garden or sit around the house watching television or whatever!

I do not want to generalise but women are more prone to expensive clothing than men and that is the reason why the bulk of clothing advertising is targeting woman.

It is as if woman can not resist the expensive clothing advertisements, in all forms and formats, zeroing in on them especially when it is brand name shoes and hand bags!

Watch this opposite repeat!

I do not want to generalise but men are more prone to expensive automobiles than women and that is the reason why the bulk of the motoring advertising is targeting men.

It is as if men can not resist the expensive vehicle advertisements, in all forms and formats, zeroing in on them especially when it is brand name very expensive four by fours!

Dear working people of this beautiful world stop complaining about the rich getting richer and the poor getting poorer because we, the working masses, are making them rich and richer!

4.1.5 Cost of Medical Aid

With the very high cost of any medical treatment all over the world it is of the utmost importance to have a sound medical aid scheme to assist you in weathering this high expenditure(Minus Money) which you will have to pay at some or another time. Everybody will get sick or go for medical treatment in a hospital, have an expensive operation at various stages in there lives.

There are countries where the state medical schemes are well managed and funded from state funds, derived from their tax systems and thus their citizens pay the minimum additional, or in some cases absolutely nothing, towards a heath system.

In a country like South Africa the state assistance with all medical aspects is a disaster thus your private medical aid must be sufficient to allow you to go to a private medical practitioner and private hospitals as the state hospitals are not conducive for high quality healthcare!

If you do not live in a country where medical aid is sufficiently covered by the state then you have no choice but to have a medical aid on which to lean when the time comes!

As mentioned in the previous section "<u>Enumeration or Salary</u>" you must ensure that your employer have a proper and decent medical aid scheme which is to you and your family's advantage e.g.

- A medical fund contribution of which is partly paid by the employer and partly by you and which in most countries are compulsory by law. (deducted from your salary per payment period)
- A sick leave system which in most countries are compulsory by law.

If you are self employed you must still have a proper and decent medical aid scheme which is to you and your family's advantage. High medical costs, especially where hospitalisation and operations are required, can be a disaster to you, your family and your business.

Medical aid generally is expensive and will be an expenditure(Minus money) and it is then very important to include into you budget!

In various countries the cost of medical aid and a medical practitioner's prescribed medicines and treatment are tax deductable or partially deductable-this aspect will be dealt with in more detail in my section on "Taxation" later on in this book.

4.1.6 Insurance

Retirement Annuities.

As stated and emphasised in various sections of this book it is of the utmost importance to save for your retirement and to start as soon and as young as possible.

One of the vehicles to save for your future is to take out a retirement annuity.

Nowadays most insurance companies have coupled products where for instance retirement annuities can be taken with, life cover and disability cover.

But what is an annuity, life and disability cover-and let's look at these.

An annuity policy is simply a personalised pension fund which you pay and manage yourself. There are usually no money contributions from your government or employer

Life cover you take to protect your family in the event that you may pass away and for the sole reason as to protect them against the monetary loss which your death will bring whether you are employed or self employed.

Disability cover you take out for if and when you are at some stage disabled to the extent where you are not able to execute your profession whether working for an employer or running your own business.

From the above sections and paragraphs it is clear that it is very necessary to have a retirement annuity, life and disability cover for your retirement and safe keeping of you and your family.(Remember that anybody can be nominated as beneficiaries as in your final will and testament)

A very important aspect that must be recognised, even before you cover yourself with insurance is that it must be Affordable. It must fit into your budget so as to prevent you from investigating yourself in to bankruptcy!

Most insurers have an automatic policy growth system whereby you decide with what percentage your payment must be increased per month after each year as to make provision for inflation and then also for a greater payment to your retirement at retirement age.

Thus, because most people get yearly increases at work or make more profit in their businesses each year I shall strongly recommend that you start with an affordable sum at the beginning of the retirement annuity and place a growth rate of 10 to 20%(percent) on it.

To get the maximum value out of an annuity it must be treated with a high level of discipline. If you do not pay it regularly and keep the payments up to date you will lose the policy and most of the money which you have paid. If you take the policy before maturity you will also lose most of your money due to the insurer's commissions and administration costs.

I shall strongly recommend that the payment for your annuity be paid by stop order then there are no chance of forgetting to do the monthly payment or that any other expenditure gets preference. Plan your policy in such a way that you can keep payments up until maturity or your retirement, whichever is latest. The reason for this is that the policy only start to gain real value after approximately ten years but then start to grow exponentially.(At a very steep rate)

Plan your retirement and work that plan with your main planning tool namely your budget.

Be aware that your policy or retirement annuity contract might give you an estimated, indicative value of what the retirement total pay out sum will be. The policy holder, you, must make sure which administration, commissioning and other cost implications will be at maturity or retirement. Very few insurers venture to contractually bind themselves to a guaranteed payout value.

Every body with retirement policies must ensure that they know of what the procedures and laws of your country is when payout occurs so as to avoid last minute surprises e.g.

In South Africa it is a law that your annuity is not paid to you in a lump sum but is reinvested and the insurer pays you a monthly pension for life. After your death your nominated family members or beneficiaries may decide to take the lump sum or continue receiving the monthly pension.

The policy holder must then ensure that the nominated family members or other beneficiaries are clearly stated in the policy and your final will and testament.

You must make sure of what the taxation laws in your country, governing pension funds, are.

In South Africa the first R120,000-00 of the annuity is exempt from taxation but the rest is taxable by the state thus make sure from the insurer AND your tax office/authority of what the particular "Tax Laws" are, concerning all of your pensioning pay outs.

There are, in most countries positive affects on your tax situation which will be mentioned in the later chapter under the heading "Taxation".

Make very sure and let it be very clear in your mind of what you want as a retirement annuity or other retirement vehicle and that you get what you want!

Shop a round, use only reputable, well known, well established and trustworthy insurance practitioners and compare different insurer's quotations with each other until you find one which is up to your expectations.

Read your policy over and over until you understand all the conditions in that that policy.

If there are conditions and sections of the policy which is not clear let the insurer explain these in detail and if you are still not satisfied talk to a lawyer or your bank manager.

I again want to reiterate that this book is as much aimed at woman as for men, and maybe even more important to women!

Although I treat your retirement annuity as an expenditure it must be noted that it is only an expenditure until you retire or when it matures-Why?

As soon as the policy pays out you don't have to pay the instalments anymore and that money, if you then save it, move from the expenditure (Minus Money) to income (Plus Money) side of your budget!

<u>Other Insurances.</u>

There are various other insurances which are very necessary to save guard you against monetary disaster and loss such as Loss of Income Cover, Home/House Contents Insurance, Car/Vehicle Insurance, Home/House Structural Insurance cover, etc., etc., etc.

The same principals as for choosing an annuity or retirement policy will apply here namely:

Shop around to get the best deal, make sure what you are buying and above all make sure that it is affordable!

With the "Home/House Contents Insurance", "Car/Vehicle Insurance", "Home/House Structural Insurance cover, make very sure of what the "excess payments will be in case of your insurance claim. The insurance companies do there homework and through statistical analysis know that most claims can be covered or partly covered by you, the consumer, by making you pay the so called excess amount when you lodge a claim. In many cases the excess amount is more than what the actual damage or item cost are. Thus thy make you pay for what you already paid and in some cases make a double profit of what you double paid!

Other that your retirement policy the chances are very good that you will not get very high returns on the money that you invest in these assurances, it is solely an expenditure to cover you against losing to much money when disaster strikes-thus it is nothing more than an evil necessity!

The most ridicules aspect of buying furniture, appliances and clothing on credit is that over and above the high cost of interest the supplier usually has a insurance payment as a standard which you pay for. What is this insurance you pay for? It is easy profit for the supplier because they already have insurance for the items while still in store, the warranty or guaranty they give you covers bad workmanship and malfunctioning, which is compensated in their selling price and the items which is damaged or stolen from or in your house is covered by your house insurances.

By buy unnecessary on credit we pay over and over for the same thing.

4.1.7 Cost of Children

I am amazed at how, all over the world, children get little or no attention as a major expenditure.

All over the world thousands of high profile conferences are regularly held on subjects such as "Sustainable Growth", "Renewable Energy" (Which just don't exist and never will), "Earth Warming", "The High Crime Rates" (Which, in South Africa is always or mostly blamed on poverty), "World Economic Conferences" etc., etc, but I have never heard of regular major world level conferences on "Over Population"-Why?

The answer is very simple. Whether capitalist, communist, democrat, republican, nationalist or whatever, over population means cheap labour, high consumer expenditure, for these populations, thus higher income and profit for the manufacturers, financiers, retail stores, agents, speculators, oil companies, directors and owners of companies- I can go on forever!

It also provides huge amounts of soldiers and other personnel for defence forces which is the single most expensive expenditure for most countries whether in peace time or at war and this expenditure is paid for by its citizens by means of .taxation, thus higher income and profit for the manufacturers, financiers, retail stores, agents, speculators, oil companies, directors and owners of companies-who gladly supply these defence forces!

But where am I going with this paragraph?

With over population come more and more poor people, because the supply in the population growth outstrips job creation and places a massive burden on governments to supply social grants, social services like medical services, infrastructure, education and so on.

Poor people without jobs do not pay for the above because they do not pay tax, the productive population pay for it!

I know to call a child an expenditure is crude but we must be realistic.

The moral of this paragraph is "Plan Your Children and their future" as to give them the best possible chances in life!

Plan them into your budget as an expenditure and at least it will guide you as to which non essentials can be discarded as to allow you to have children who will have a reasonable successful financial chance in life!

I can assure you that if children are not planned there will be major monitory implications-so plan and budget even at the stage where you start thinking of having children!

Read all your insurance policies and thrash out the SMALL PRINT with the insurer even to the point where you want written signed sealed and stamped confirmation of the aspects which is not clear to you or to what you want and do not want!

Before Child Birth

Even before the birth of your child your expenditure will become greater as pre-birth medical care is essential for the child to be born safely and healthy.

There will be extra doctors fees, continuous specialist fees, various blood and other prenatal tests, baby clothing, a cot, various other furniture and the cost of preparing for a special baby room.

Child Birth

If you do not live in one of those well governed countries where the state hospitals are highly professional and medical care is "free", not really so free because you already paid for it via your taxation system, you must know that the costs of a birth are very expensive. Hospitalisation, doctors, specialists, anaesthetists and post birth medical treatment will be expensive!

You must have medical insurance and if you have, make sure that you are covered for the birth. Read your insurance policy or contract and make sure that child birth, pre and post birth is covered. Make sure at what stage, if not already covered in your insurance policy or contract, the child must be covered as a dependant-do not just assume that your medical aid always covers every aspect of your medical needs. Read your medical policy and thrash out the SMALL PRINT with the insurer even to the point where you want written signed sealed and stamped confirmation of the aspects which is not clear to you or to what you want and do not want!

Cost of Education

If your are married and you are in the situation where the wife must work out of necessity or due to career obligations, you must know that provision must be made for day care and pre school expenses. This is where the child's schooling expenditure really start and the child schooling expenditure must be incorporated into your BUDGET

Refer the table below for an estimated average cost to get your child through school from pre-school to completion of a college diploma or university degree.

Estimated Schooling Expenditure

	SA Rand Per Year	U.S. Dollar Per Year	British Pound Per Year	Escalated @ Years 15%Rand	Escalated @ Years 15%USD	Escalated @ Years 15%Pound
Pre School 2 Years	7,200	689	408	15,480	1,481	878
Primary School 5 Years	12,000	1,143	680	80,909	7,735	4,587
High School 5 Years	14,000	1,333	793	107878	9,024	5,351
Technical College 3 Years	16,000	1,523	907	107,878	10,313	6,115
University 3 Years	40,000	3,810	2,268	269,695	25,783	15,288
University 5 Years e.g. Medical (7 But 2 internship with salary)	55,000	5,238	3,118	370,831	35,452	21,022
Total Schooling up to Grade 12				204,267	18,240	10,816
Total Schooling up to Technical College				312,145	28,553	16,931
Total				473,962	44,023	26,104

Schooling up to University General Total			
Schooling up to University Medical	575,098	53,692	31,838

To make provision for Accommodation, Clothing, Transport, Text Books, Stationary, Food, Daily Personal and Hygiene Care and General

Spending Money, Cell/Mobile phone and other general expenses at least twenty percent (20%) must be added if you plan to send your child to college or university.

Thus the estimated Cost for an After School Education will escalate to:

Monetary Unit	South African Rand	United States Dollar	British Pound
Total Schooling up to Technical College	374,574	34,264	20,317
Total Schooling up to University General	568,754	52,828	31,325
Total Schooling up to University Medical	690,118	64,430	38,206

Special Notes:

All tuition costs are based on an estimated average in South African Institutions.

The Base Date for my estimates is April 12, 2014.

The costs are rounded to nearest monetary unit

As we can see a high level of schooling is at a high price and will increase to higher prices.

So it is of the utmost importance that parents be prepared for this expenditure and budget for it.

It is also important for parents to no how to minimize the cost of education by investigating various institutions of learning long before making final decisions.

Various colleges, universities, government departments and various companies offer bursaries for high achieving students with good passes in their grades.

Usually bursaries offered by businesses and government departments also assure the student a working position after college or university, or for that matter any tertiary institution, and if the student passed they do not have the to pay back the bursary but, alternatively, work the time of at the business or government department. Just make sure that the contract is to your satisfaction and that you and your child or dependant understands the contract.

Another method of minimizing the cost of obtaining a tertiary education is to make use of distance learning. Most institutions of higher learning have distance learning departments which allows the student to study from home, cutting accommodation, travel and various other costs.

This method demands a high degree of discipline and good administration from the student but it will also give him or her an advantage in later working or business life.

In South Africa we are fortunate to have UNISA(The University of South Africa) one of the biggest and best, if not the biggest and best, distance learning universities in the world which not only caters for S.A. students but have tens of thousands of students from all over the world and is exclusively a distance learning institution.

Some countries give a tax deduction if your child study at a higher education institution-this is also a possible expenditure reduction method that must be investigated.

In closing this section I want to emphasise that an education for you and your children is of the utmost importance.

Whether aspiring to become an engineer, accountant, motor mechanic, electrician or school teacher you must make sure that you get, through hard work and study, your trade qualification documents, diploma or degree and study even further.

Make sure you do not force yourself and or your children into a direction of study just for the money or prestige. I am definitely not an educationist at all but one must determine the main ability and interest of oneself and your children.

There are many ways to find out what the best direction is to study in e.g.

Find out what you and or your children are interested in through communication and observation. Find out what yourself and or your children talk about, what games are played and what is read.

Take note of the aptitude testing which is done throughout primary and high school and if there weren't, aren't any done find out where it can be done-most colleges, universities and private institutions can be utilised

Take note of Career Guidance Classes as taught and presented by schools, colleges and universities which will enlighten anybody of which direction to study.

The reader must take cognisance of the fact that many individuals became millionaires with little or no schooling but by using their intelligence, plain common sense, hard work, persistence, discipline, contentiousness, passion and above all taking a keen interest in what you want, or like to do.

Good schooling gives you a distinct advantage when starting of with any career.

There are many individuals who do not just want to chase money and become millionaires but rather want to have a solid and interesting career and if they then follow this with passion it will bring them to an amiable, comfortable, sound financial life and retirement position.

Every person must qualify himself to be able to save money wisely and budget to control both the income and expenditure so as to prepare for a stress free life and retirement.

4.1.8 Cost of Banking/Savings

Most people make use of banking institutions in one or another form. Your salary, pension monthly payouts, business income and various other incomes are paid into one or more of your bank accounts. Out of your banking accounts your expenditures are being paid, your home, car/vehicle, groceries, water, electricity, savings and various other expenditures, either by debit orders, cheque payments, debit cards, credit cards, internet banking, cash withdrawals and bank transfers.

Very few people on earth know or even care that the banks makes money out of every single transaction that you make or that is being done automatically and for whatever transaction.

So it is of the utmost importance that you know what your bank is doing with your money!

So it is of the utmost importance that you know what your bank is doing with your bank Charges or in other words your Baking Costs!

Choosing a Bank

When choosing a bank or financial institution you must ensure that it is reputable and controlled by either your country's banking laws and regulations and or banking regulators.

Make sure that the cost of banking is as low as you can possibly find and then negotiate with the bank for even lower bank costs and where possible insist on fixed bank rates which are acceptable to you.

The main banking costs, as based in South Africa is, and amongst others are Administration Fees, Transaction Fees, Internet Banking Fees, Rewards Fees, Credit Card Fees, Debit

Card Fees, Debit Order Fees, Cheque Transaction Fees Cheque Book Fees.

Check Your Monthly Bank Statements.

It is very important to always check your monthly bank statements simply because some of the of the banking transactions are done by human data capturers and simply by being human they make mistakes and either double charge or over charge you on various transactions.

The bank's computer systems are also programmed, maintained and changed by human beings

So constantly check the interest rates on your Overdraft , Internet Banking , Credit Card , Debit Card, Cheque, Home Bond, Car/Vehicle and your Savings accounts.

Constantly check Administration Fees, Transaction Fees, Internet Banking Fees, Rewards Fees, Credit Card Fees, Debit Card Fees, Debit Order Fees, Cheque Transaction Fees, Cheque Book Fees Home Bond and Car/Vehicle fees.

4.1.9 Cost of Investments

Take care not to over invest to the extent where you threaten the other priorities in you and your family's lives.

About twenty five years ago I found that my budget was going into the negative, that is my expenditure(Minus Money) were greater that my income(Plus Money).

On analysing my budget I found that I had three annuities and one study policy with my insurance company.

By making the one policy paid up I not only balanced my budget but also went into the plus money situation which gave me room to save more and pay house of quicker.

4.1.10 Stock Market/Share Trading

As previously discussed, if you want to challenge the stock market prepare yourself to know as much about this investment area as you can. Start your investments with small amounts, investigate the companies in which you wish to invest, first buy small caps at the lowest price and sell as soon as these show a profit.

It is advisable to make use of a stock broker but do not let him talk you into investing to large amounts to soon and always do your own homework.

The stock market can be a very good financial vehicle or it can be an outright money death trap!

Other "So Called Investments"

The world of investment criminal's inventions, the so called "Con Jobs", is as old as history itself!

Always remember the saying "If something sounds to good to be true, it always isn't true"!

A person immaculately dressed, these people usually are, approached me with an offer of buying R100,000-00 plus minus $US 10,000-00, into a company which guarantees a 47% yearly interest on my investment.

I asked him why he, himself, doesn't invest his own money into this company with such a fantastic, fabulous interest rate.

He smiled at me turned around and walked away.

Investigate all investments in depth before investing.

Taxation

4.1.11 Paying Tax

There are numerous "musts" in this life and on this earth such as-one must eat, drink, go to the toilette, have cloths to wear, have a place to live, grow old and die.

If you live in a modern civilised country with a government and earn an income it is a "must" to pay income tax on the money earned.

Taxation is, as such, then an expenditure or minus money and the government of that country must return that money in the form of total social services to the people of the particular country.

Paying your taxes allow governments, and they are obliges to do so, to return that money in the form of police and defence forces which keeps you safe, schools, health services such as hospitals, universities, infrastructure like a road and rail system, dams for water, airports and a variety of services that its citizens are entitled to.

So every citizen earning money must pay income tax in some form or format!

I shall very strongly advise any person with any taxation liability to make sure that your taxes are being paid. If you are an employee of a company make sure that your employer deduct the taxes and enough of it within the limits of your country's tax laws.

The reason is very simple in that the most efficient departments in all countries are the Tax or government Revenue collection departments. They employ the best of accountants, actuaries, auditors and other highly skilled personnel to ensure that the government gets your tax money.

Make very sure that you know exactly what your tax account rights and liabilities are and why. It is very simple because in most tax disputes the tax offices first investigate the individual and then the company and then the employment or labour agency or broker responsible for paying over the tax amount over to the tax department(Where P.A.Y.E, Pay As You Earn, Applies)

Let me give you and example of a tax misfortune that happened to me.

From 1989 to 1999 I was employed by a company who, for my last two year period, decided that all non executive personnel will be reemployed on a long term contract basis. A labour broker was used to manage all our terms and conditions including our tax obligations. To cut a long story short is that when I left this company and I had to get tax clearances for my pension and provident funds, an audit by the tax department revealed that the labour broker never paid over the correct amounts to my tax account-they simply paid just ninety percent and stuffed ten percent into their own pockets!

My first reaction was to request the tax office's auditor to retrieve the money from the labour broker upon which the particular tax office accountant stated that they did their "home work" and that the broker emigrated to Brazil so I personally, was liable for paying the shortfall as South Africa had no extradition or other law enforcement treaties with Brazil.

When consulting a specialist tax lawyer he advised me to pay the tax office the outstanding amount immediately as to avoid any further lawyer fees, interest and penalties which will just increase the amount due.

He also advised me that in future I must make sure that I personally see to it that my tax dues are paid, by continuously checking when it is due and that it is in accordance with the tax laws of my country.

He also stressed that the tax law of South Africa clearly demands that for the individual citizen's tax obligations, the individual is finally responsible for the payment of taxes and outstanding amounts unless proven otherwise.(Of coarse the "proven otherwise" is definitely going to cost you huge amounts of tax lawyer's or other tax expert's fees

In total I lost R125,725-00(plus minus $ US 12,572-00) in Tax back payment, interest and revenue service penalties. Taken that I then also lost interest on this amount, if I could have saved it, the amount lost would have accumulated to approximately R 28,300-00(plus minus $ 2,830-00 US 00). In 1999 to me this was a lot of money to lose!

So each individual must make absolutely sure that he or she has total control and have in depth knowledge of what is required for paying tax and that it is each Individual's, Business's or other entity's <u>Responsibility!</u>

Otherwise, the tax situation can .be a nasty and unexpected expenditure and minus money, negatively influencing your whole budgeted situation.

Make sure that you know what the different types of Taxation exists e.g.:

VAT; Value Added Tax;

PAYE; Pay As You Earn;

Tax on Share/Stock Holding;

Carbon Tax; and

CGT, Capital Gains Tax.

Make sure that you know where these different types, and other and other forms of Taxations are applied whether for private or business income.

Tax Returns and Deductions.

But paying your taxes can also be a sort of a saving contributor if you just think of it clearly and bring yourself to a point where you know what your tax rights and obligations are.

The first step is to realise that the roads you travel on, the government schools, hospitals and all the other services your government supply, or must supply, are being paid with the tax money you pay to the government. Due to the tax that you pay you do not have to pay for the facilities that your government supply, as described in the previous section, using your tax money.

What you must also know is that there are, in most countries, a variety of deductions and rebates that can be claimed against the tax amounts that you pay.

In South Africa there are a variety of rebates and deductions that can be claimed for instance, some of your medical aid contributions, your private vehicle travelling if and when it is being used for business travel, a pensioner's deductions and other various other deductions.

If you had proper investments for retirement it is advisable to consult with your bank's financial/tax consultant, insurance broker/institution, tax lawyer and your local tax office to what tax deductions and rebates can be claimed and which you are, by law entitled to.

In South Africa, for instance, there are various tax incentives for certain investments on retirement which is tax free or partly tax free e.g. R 34,500-00 in your saving or other bank, unit trust, stockbrokers and various other accounts.

Always consider always increasing the amounts you save-Why, simply because every amount you save is simply a saving and thus PLUS Money!

For instance in South Africa, from March 2015, you will be allowed to save up to 27.5% of your income, tax free and you will be able to withdraw R500,000-00 tax free on retirement! That is, in my opinion a brilliant move from our government as this is a huge incentive for the individual to save and to assist the government to ease state pension pay outs and grants to the elderly who did not or could not provide for their own retirement.

The bottom line is that every individual must make sure that he or she has enough knowledge of their tax system to know exactly what the individual's or your business's rights and obligations are.

Although this book is written with a South African basis the basic elements will apply in the majority of countries.

Bottom lines on the subject of paying compulsory government tax is to know your obligations so as not losing additional tax money due to outstanding liabilities upon which you have to pay interest on outstanding amounts and other penalties.

Know your countries income tax system as to know what you must pay, what you are paying and above all what rebates/refunds and incentives there are as for you or your business to, legally, get money back from the tax system.

4.1.12 Cost of Non essentials

Again I want to emphasise that one must be disciplined with money and respect it. Do not buy anything which is not really needed or that you are not going to use-why buy anything if there is no use for it and it will either rot or contribute to cluttering your packing space! There are companies which make billions by selling cupboards, closets, shelving, plastic containers, steel mesh containers, plastic zip bags with vacuum compression e.tc,.etc to the masses of this earth to store, pack and cram in all their clutter! The business world conditions the masses to "Shop Till They Drop" and then make them pay for places and spaces to store what they bought!

5 Closing

In closing I want to repeat, in a very short way, what has already been said in my book but what need be repeated so as to put a final emphasis on certain aspects.

5.1 Hindsight.

Everybody knows the age old saying "Hindsight is an Exact Science" and it is an exact science which everybody has experienced, is experiencing and will experience.

We older persons know the mistakes we made, the opportunities we missed, good decisions we made and the lessons we learned and the corrective actions we took and had to take!

So investigate, study and learn every aspect of money from everybody and everything what you can.

One of the most important lessons of money that I have learned is like with everything in our lives-"Prevention is better than Cure".

5.2 Your Budget.

Draw up your budget as detailed as possible, truthfully as possible, constantly update it, take detailed notice of the truth it will tell you, act upon the truth it tells you and in the short , medium and long term you and your family will benefit from it.

5.3 Do not Compete with the Joneses.

Many years ago I saw a cartoon in a financial publication depicting a man holding a printing machine with bundles of U.S. Dollars bulging from every pocket of his pants and jacket and sided by two grumpy looking policemen.

The next door neighbour and his wife were watching the scene over the fence and the caption of the cartoon was "And that my dear wife is the Joneses we have been competing with!" What a lesson in a cartoon.

Because you do not have a clue of what other people's financial statuses are, do not compete with them because you simply do not know what you are competing against!

Live your own truth full monetary life and be happy.

5.4 Fantastic Money Making Schemes and MICRO Lending

Remember that if something looks to good to be true it most probably isn't true.

Before you make investments in anything, study the investment.

Ask your bank's financial advisors, lawyer, older people, the internet, the general media of what the risks of these investments are.

Tens of thousands of people in South Africa has fallen foul and lost millions of their savings, pension payouts and inheritances due to investing in dubious property developments, cheap vehicle deals, so called high interest rate return "banking" investments and where the so called owners of these companies hardly have enough money to print there dubious brochures and pay there dubious sales force. Once these companies siphoned tens of millions from pensioners and other financial naïve and careless people they shamelessly make the money "disappear" and they themselves "disappear" to a country which do not have an extradition agreement with the country where the conned investors "invested" their money.

5.5 Gambling

In 1970 I was lucky to get a reasonably prices holiday going on a cruise ship in the Indian ocean.

Because it was very quiet and relaxing I, every evening before dinner, had a drink in the cruise ship's gambling room.

I noticed a man who virtually every evening won considerable amounts of money at the poker tables and although the players changed most evenings he was always there and playing at the same table.

On our cruise liner reaching Mauritius there was an announcement that a special tour for visiting the casino on this beautiful island was organised.

There was considerable excitement among all South Africans as, at that stage there were no casinos allowed in our country.

I approached the man who had the winning streak in the gambling room for some "tips" and two of my last questions were "What system can I use and how much money should I take going to the casino?"

He smiled and answered "Not even good professional gamblers have systems that can assure winning in most casinos so only take the amount of money that you are prepared to lose and enjoy the visit and have an evening of fun."

One must realise that all gambling institutions are there to make money and not to dish it out!

Whether Casinos, Horse Racing, Lotto or any other form of gambling institution, these have huge liabilities on their premises, computers, machines, staff salaries massive overheads of water, electricity and share holder payment which is "Massive Expenditures".

They simply make their millions to cover these expenditures and huge profits by, as an estimate, ensure that 10,000 people lose small money for every one that win small money and make 5,000 lose big money for every one that wins big money.

So it is better not to gamble at all as the odds will always be stacked against you.

In South Africa your chance of winning the Lotto is approximately 1 out of 15,000,000 and the Power Ball approximately 1 out of 35,000,000 which is virtually No Chance or Probability.

By all means gamble for fun but use the minimum of money and lady luck might just be on your side.

Whether you gamble small or big money your chances will be the same, as the luck of the draw and the gambling institutions will ultimately decide between winning and losing!

5.6 Laws

Make sure that you have insight and knowledge of the laws of your country, local government, state, province and local government bylaws as these will have various taxes and tariffs which will be for your account and will be enforced to be paid by you. Take note of these and ensure that it is budgeted in your budget as expenditure.

5.7 Micro Lenders.

In South Africa there are a myriad of banking institutions and small operators who trade in small loans for the general public and it can be acquired by very short noticed approval, with very little or no collateral. Some of these operators are known as "Loan Sharks"-but why?

There are several of these operators who charge criminally high interest rates, binding their clients with very complicated contracts, which the client hardly ever read or understand. The institution's contract forces the client to open an account with them where the client's salary gets paid into that bank account with a preferential stop order on the client's salary for the payback of this loan.

Risk

Most micro lending has a very high risk factor in that these high interest rates and complicated contracts will not only push you into deeper debt but also that it takes control of your salary and thus destabilise your money base.

A big risk is also that a lot of these institutions do not have sound banking regulatory, risk analysis and risk preventative systems and then pose a high risk of going into liquidation. A point in case is the African Bank collapsing and leaving the South African reserve bank to bale it out, leaving share holders, tax payers and other individuals out of money and even discredited the country's banking system and South Africa. The people who borrowed money from these institutions are now going to be more out of pocket due to the collapse and probable liquidation because the costs of credit collection, law, accounting firms and administration personnel will simply be passed to the shareholders and borrowers-by hook or by crook!

The owners, management and directors most probably walked away with their bank accounts, in other safe and reputable banks, stuffed full of money and as reported by the South African media not caring much of what they left behind.

As reported by the media Abil's "chief risk officer", of all chief officers, Tami Sokutu when being interviewed on the legacy left behind simply stated and I quote

" F**** the poor I'm going to play golf in Scotland"!

According to the Sunday Times[1] News paper, Sokutu, who made over R50million in share options and earned another R35million in salary and bonuses while he was Abil's chief risk officer, showed no sign of remorse for the reckless lending to millions of South African's who could not afford to repay their debt. This, say analysts, has led to the collapse of the bank.

During his interview with the newspaper he reportedly boasted about having made millions and said he was now globetrotting.

Sokutu reportedly owns three houses in South Africa and another in Portugal.

He said he did not need to ever work again and according to him he also owns six luxury cars, including a Porsche and a Bentley.

He said he lived a lavish lifestyle and had no regrets and blamed borrowers for their predicament and said they should not have applied for loans if they were not able to repay them.

South African Reserve Bank governor Gill Marcus last Sunday announced that African Bank had been placed under curatorship.

---

1.   http://www.pressreader.com/south-africa/sunday-times/textview

The bottom line here is to not make use of, or invest in these institutions-it will be to your monetary detriment!

5.8 But how can money give one "Freedom"?

There are many meanings and interpretations of the word freedom e.g. Liberty, Self-determination, Independence, Choice, and various others.

I shall distinctly differentiate between the different types of freedoms, for instance political freedom, freedom of association, personal freedom, freedom to eat what I want, to listen to the music I prefer e.t.c.

To explain my concept of "money freedom" I shall make the following distinction between political and money freedom.

There are a very high percentage of nations and peoples who have political freedom by which they have their own country, own government and governing institutions and have the right to vote.

But within these countries there are hundreds of millions of people, who do not eat a decent meal per day, who do not have decent clothes to wear or have a proper bed to sleep in, never mind a house to live in all because they do not have money and mostly not of their own doing but because they do not have monetary freedom!

There are millions of people who do eat three high cost meals per day, who do have decent and brand name clothes to wear, have an expensive bed to sleep in, a fabulous house to live in and two expensive cars in the garage but do not have a peaceful sleep or night's rest all because they do have money but do not manage it so as to maintain this lifestyle-they live on credit thus on Minus money and are not free!

Of all the meanings of freedom I shall pick three to end my book namely:

Choice-So as to skilfully choose how I am going to use my money to carry me throughout my life; and

Self-determination so as to secure my monetary Independence for peace of mind and future prosperity!

If one is able to make the right personal monetary/financial choices, at an early stage, and add determination this book might just be the stepping stone to becoming rich!

Don't miss out!

Visit the website below and you can sign up to receive emails whenever Gert van Niekerk publishes a new book. There's no charge and no obligation.

https://books2read.com/r/B-A-ZQTS-KGOXB

BOOKS 2 READ

Connecting independent readers to independent writers.